Best Easy Day Hikes
Northeast New Jersey

Help Us Keep This Guide Up to Date

Every effort has been made by the authors and editors to make this guide as accurate and useful as possible. However, many things can change after a guide is published—trails are rerouted, regulations change, facilities come under new management, etc.

We would love to hear from you concerning your experiences with this guide and how you feel it could be improved and kept up to date. While we may not be able to respond to all comments and suggestions, we'll take them to heart and we'll also make certain to share them with the authors. Please send your comments and suggestions to the following address:

Globe Pequot Press
Reader Response/Editorial Department
P.O. Box 480
Guilford, CT 06437

Or you may e-mail us at:

editorial@GlobePequot.com

Thanks for your input, and happy trails!

Best Easy Day Hikes Series

Best Easy Day Hikes
Northeast New Jersey

Paul E. DeCoste
Ronald J. Dupont Jr.

FALCONGUIDES

GUILFORD, CONNECTICUT
HELENA, MONTANA

AN IMPRINT OF GLOBE PEQUOT PRESS

FALCONGUIDES®

Copyright © 2010 by Morris Book Publishing, LLC

Falcon, FalconGuides, and Outfit Your Mind are registered trademarks
of Morris Book Publishing, LLC.

Project editor: Julie Marsh
Layout artist: Kevin Mak
Maps: Design Maps Inc. © Morris Book Publishing, LLC

Library of Congress Cataloging-in-Publication Data
DeCoste, Paul E.
  Best easy day hikes northeast New Jersey / Paul E. DeCoste,
Ronald J. Dupont Jr.
      p. cm.
  Includes bibliographical references and index.
  ISBN 978-0-7627-5437-3 (alk. paper)
 1. Hiking–New Jersey–Guidebooks. 2. New Jersey–Guidebooks. I.
Dupont, Ronald J. II. Title.
  GV199.42.N5D42 2010
  796.5109749–dc22

                                        2009034240

Printed in the United States of America
10 9 8 7 6 5 4 3 2 1

As I sit on the top rock of Winbeam, I think: It is good to *know* a place, and to *love* it. To look as far as the eye can reach, and know where every road and trail begins and ends—to know every hidden nook in this valley where you'll find each flower and herb in its season . . . Yes, it is good to know a place, the place where you began life, to know its people and history. It is good for you, whether you live there all the time, or come to visit there, or if you are treasuring it in the shrine of loving memory.

Minnie Mae Monks, *Winbeam* (1930)

May you all know and love this special part of the world.

Contents

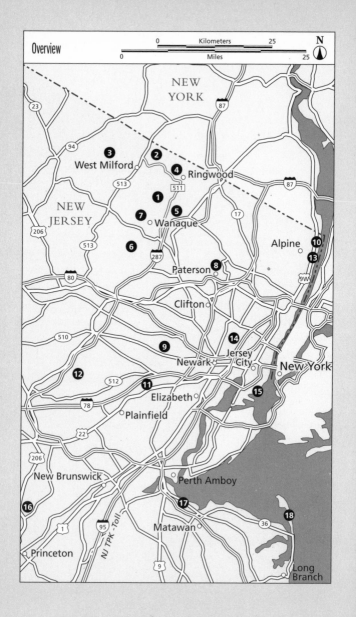

Acknowledgments

Firstly, we give our deep and multiple thanks to our patient project editor, Julie Marsh, and our even more patient editor, Scott Adams.

A number of these hikes were adapted from our larger book, *Hiking New Jersey* (FalconGuides 2009). The folks who assisted us in the writing of that book we also thank here.

As always, we offer thanks to our wives, Pat DeCoste and Emilie Dupont, for their help and assistance in this endeavor. Emilie read the draft and provided many useful comments. Pat hiked the hikes and provided invaluable office support.

Introduction

Northeast New Jersey is a wonderful place for a walk. And for some folks, that may come as a surprise.

Let's say it up front: The Jersey 'burbs aren't most people's idea of hiking heaven. The region is smack in the middle of the great Northeastern Megalopolis that stretches (at least) from Massachusetts to Virginia, and is thus sometimes called BosWash (Boston to Washington). Urban and suburban sprawl of the twentieth century has made it basically one long city of fifty-five million people.

As such, there are a whole lotta people around here. The seven New Jersey counties that make up the stomping grounds for these hikes have a combined population of 4.6 million people, nearly 3,000 people per square mile. That exceeds the population of twenty-seven other entire *states*. Hudson County has more people in its 62 square miles than Wyoming does in its 98,000. In short, it's the most densely populated area of the most densely populated state in the nation. We're talking population density higher than that of Bangladesh, India, or China.

And yet it's indeed a great place for a hike. Those who don't live here, and many who do, will be surprised to find a tremendous amount of open spaces and recreational resources. There are forests, peaks, waterfalls, lakes, rivers, ponds, old mines, historic ruins—all within an hour of Times Square.

How did this happen? The residents of this urban juggernaut have always valued their parks, from lower Manhattan's Bowling Green in the 1730s to Central Park in the 1850s and New Jersey's Branch Brook Park in the 1890s.

1

New Jersey has one of the oldest state park systems in the nation, established in 1905. For generations, New Jersey has had progressive and intelligent programs for acquiring and improving open space. Today that commitment shows, and it contributes to our quality of life.

These parks run the gamut from areas like the Palisades, beloved open space for a century, to the additions of more recent decades, like Liberty State Park and Pyramid Mountain Natural Area. Some serve up New York metro ambience, while others give you a real taste of the wild. The choice is all yours.

Weather

New Jersey weather is as diverse as our landscape. Winters, especially here in the north, are akin to those in New England, with deep snows and subzero temperatures not uncommon. Winter hiking requires suitable clothing and gear. Elevation changes can make a huge difference. A light February rain in Liberty State Park can be snow at the Torne; a pleasant spring day in the Palisades can still be wintry in the Ramapos.

New Jersey summers can likewise be Southern-style hot, humid, and hazy, with temperatures peaking over 100 degrees at times. Sunscreen and water are essentials. Many times of year are bug-free in New Jersey, but not all. If one Jersey joke has merit, it's the one about the state bird being the mosquito. The tick, once relatively uncommon, can now be a serious pest. The moral: Wear bug repellent. All times of year have their glories for the hiker—if you are prepared.

Trail Regulations/Restrictions

The hikes in this book are on a federally owned national recreation area, in state parks and forests, in county parks, in one interstate park (Palisades), and in one park run by an independent commission (DeKorte). As such, trail regulations and restrictions can and do vary depending on location and may change over time. Access to most locations is free, but some charge admission, especially in summertime. Some trails are multiuse, while others are hiker-only. Some areas permit dogs, while others prohibit them. Generally, none permit off-road vehicles, ATVs, or off-road motorcycles.

In short, it's always worth doing your homework before you hit the trail—use the contact information in this book to make sure you know what the rules are. Responsible hikers know and obey regulations, as should you. If nothing else, such preparation will avoid heading out for a peaceful tramp in the woods, only to find that the local mountain-bike chapter is having its rally that day on the trail you have chosen.

Preparing for Your Hike

A fun hike depends on being prepared. A few moments spent gathering the right stuff can spell the difference between a great stroll and an unpleasant one—or worse. Bring a daypack. Your basic kit should include:

- **Water.** More than you think you'll need. You may need it.

- **Food.** Lunch, a snack, or some gorp. Food is good. With both food and water, each hiker should carry his or her own, in the event they get separated.

- **The right clothes,** for example, a hat for sunny days, raingear for cloudy ones, extra clothing for cold weather (e.g. a wool or Polarfleece sweater), etc. An ounce of preparation is worth a lot. Never be afraid to throw a little extra gear in the pack—the weight won't kill ya. *But* in cold or wet weather, leave cotton clothes at home. When cotton gets wet, it stays wet, and it won't keep you warm. Stick with synthetics.

- **Sensible, sturdy shoes.** Try to hike the Castle Point Trail in flip-flops and you will hate life. In addition to comfort, proper shoes will help reduce injury to your feet, ankles, and knees.

- **A trail map.** This isn't optional. Trails aren't always well blazed. Find the right map for your hike and bring it! A compass is useful for orienting the map, so that's a good idea, too.

- **A cell phone,** necessary for potential emergencies. But remember: There are lots of nooks and hollows where you won't have service. And keep in mind that you, not the local police or rangers, are responsible for getting yourself out of the woods. Calls to them should be restricted to *genuine* emergencies.

- **Bug repellent and sunscreen** in warm weather. One prevents suffering now; one prevents suffering later. Bring both.

- **A watch.** If your park closes at 5 p.m. and you're lingering on the trail till 5:30, you will have one grumpy ranger to deal with at the gate.

- And lastly, of course, bring **this book.**

Other things you may want to bring along, depending on your preferences: a GPS unit, a camera, a small first-aid kit, a flashlight, a knife or multiuse tool, lighter or matches, a pen and paper, a walking stick, binoculars, and field guides. We won't pretend that all these things are vital on a short day hike, but they can come in mighty handy.

You should also learn to identify and deal with two potentially injurious pests: ticks and poison ivy. Ticks come in several varieties, the most worrisome being the tiny deer tick, which carries Lyme disease. However, all ticks can carry a variety of diseases. Insect repellent will help keep them off, and a thorough all-body check at home at day's end will remove any unwanted hitchhikers. Poison ivy is a serious nuisance in certain areas, and a bad case can mean a trip to the doctor; if you can't readily identify it, learn to (Google it!). Remember, leaves of three, let it be. If you've ever suffered through it, you know it's worth avoiding it.

Zero Impact

We, as trail users, must be vigilant to make sure our passage leaves no lasting mark. Here are some basic guidelines for preserving trails in the region:

- Pack out all your own trash. You might also pack out garbage left by less-considerate hikers.
- Don't approach or feed any wild creatures—the raccoon or crow eyeing your snack food is best able to survive if it remains self-reliant.
- Don't pick wildflowers or gather rocks, antlers, feathers, or other treasures along the trail. Removing these items will only take away from the next hiker's experience.
- Avoid damaging trailside soils and plants by remaining on the established route.

- Be courteous by not making loud noises while hiking.
- Many of these trails are multiuse, which means you'll share them with other hikers, trail runners, mountain bikers, and equestrians. Familiarize yourself with the proper trail etiquette, yielding the trail when appropriate.
- Use outhouses at trailheads or along the trail.

How to Use This Guide

Each region begins with an introduction, which provides a sweeping look at the lay of the land. After this general overview, specific hikes within that region are presented.

To aid in quick decision making, each hike chapter begins with a hike summary. These short summaries give you a taste of the hiking adventure to follow. You'll learn about the trail terrain and what surprises the route has to offer. Next, you'll find the quick, nitty-gritty details of the hike: where the trailhead is located, the nearest town, hike length, approximate hiking time, difficulty rating, best hiking seasons, type of trail terrain, what other trail users you may encounter, trail contacts (for updates on trail conditions), and trail schedules and usage fees.

The approximate hiking times are based on a standard hiking pace of 1.5 to 2 miles per hour, adjusted for terrain and reflecting normal trail conditions. The stated times will get you there and back, but be sure to add time for rest breaks and enjoying the trail's attractions. Although the stated times offer a planning guideline, you should gain a sense of your personal health, capabilities, and hiking style and make this judgment for yourself. If you're hiking with a group, add enough time for slower members. The amount of carried gear also will influence hiking speed. In all cases leave enough daylight to accomplish the task safely.

The **Finding the trailhead** section gives you dependable directions from a nearby city or town right down to where you'll want to park your car. The hike description is the meat of the chapter. Detailed and honest, it's the authors' carefully researched impression of the trail. While it's impossible to cover everything, you can rest assured that we won't miss what's important. In **Miles and Directions** we provide mileage cues to key junctions and trail name changes, as well as points of interest. The selected benchmarks allow for a quick check on progress and serve as your touchstone for staying on course.

Lastly, the **Hike Alternatives** section at the end of the book identifies hikes that didn't make the cut, for whatever reason. In some cases it's not because they aren't great hikes but because they're overcrowded or environmentally sensitive to heavy traffic. Be sure to scan this list. A jewel might be lurking among them.

Trail Finder

Best Hikes for Waterfalls, Lakes, Rivers, and Streams

Best Hikes for Geology Lovers

Best Hikes for Children

Best Hikes for Great Views, Vistas, and Skylines

Best Hikes for Industrial Archaeology and Mines

Best Hikes for Railroads

14   DeKorte Park and the Meadowlands

Best Hikes for History

Best Hikes for Unique Environmental Features

Map Legend

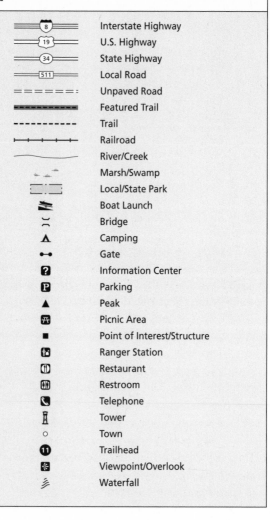

	Interstate Highway
	U.S. Highway
	State Highway
	Local Road
	Unpaved Road
	Featured Trail
	Trail
	Railroad
	River/Creek
	Marsh/Swamp
	Local/State Park
	Boat Launch
	Bridge
	Camping
	Gate
	Information Center
	Parking
	Peak
	Picnic Area
	Point of Interest/Structure
	Ranger Station
	Restaurant
	Restroom
	Telephone
	Tower
	Town
	Trailhead
	Viewpoint/Overlook
	Waterfall

The Highlands

The Highlands are the rugged heart of northern New Jersey's mountains. They are a southern extension of the New England Physiographic Province, embracing the great mountains of the Northeast. This includes some of the oldest and most geologically complex rock in New Jersey. Broad, rounded, flat-topped parallel mountain ridges separate narrow, steep-walled valleys, running northeast–southwest. The mountains are covered in dense forest, punctuated here and there by extensive swamps.

The Highlands have a northern and a southern face. Ten thousand years ago the Wisconsin glacier stopped about midway down the Jersey Highlands, roughly where I-80 runs today. The mile-thick ice sheet retreated thereafter, leaving an indistinct pile of soil and earth it plowed up. Geologists call this a terminal moraine.

South of this terminal moraine, the Highlands have a more gently rolling character and deeper soils; mountains might have farm fields on their very summit. To the north of the moraine, where our hikes are located, the ice sheet scoured the Highlands like a bulldozer, leaving behind such glacial features as bald peaks, deep valleys, steep rocky slopes, ponds and kettle lakes, and occasional huge boulders that hitchhiked south, called "erratics." This post-glacial landscape can be both harsh (especially on the feet) and beautiful.

It was certainly harsh for the early settlers who farmed here. The soils were often thin and stony, and picking rocks was an endless job. The massive stone farm fences you'll find on even a short jaunt through the Highlands forests are reminders of these ghost farms of the hills. They are the by-product of clearing such stone and laying out farm fields.

The Highlands did have a hidden treasure, though: This is where most of New Jersey's mineral wealth was located. Mines (first iron, later zinc) operated in this region from the earliest days of settlement right up through the 1970s. You will still find old mine pits and shafts, as well as the ruins of the furnaces that smelted the ore. The historic iron industry forms the backdrop for many of the state parks in the region, including Ringwood State Park, Long Pond Ironworks State Park, Allamuchy Mountain State Park, and Wawayanda State Park.

In the twentieth century the Highlands became the area where more and more people went looking for vacation spots. First hotels, then lake communities and cabin colonies sprouted on the landscape. Summer houses with charming log architecture and stone fireplaces surrounded pretty (if artificial) lakes and ponds. By the 1930s this was New Jersey's commuting-distance version of the Adirondacks.

This onetime-industrial, oft-recreational region is now earmarked for preservation. With the passage of the Highlands Water Protection and Planning Act, future development is prohibited in much of the scenic 1.2-million-acre area. The Highlands are valuable not just as scenery but also as a watershed for the Jersey cities and suburbs. The industrial history and recreational heritage embodied here will thus, with luck, be augmented by the preservation of much of the Highlands as valued open space.

1 Ball Mountain and Roomy Mine

Starting at the New Jersey Audubon Society's Weis Ecology Center, this Highlands ramble gives you a sample of the Wanaque Mountains' scenery and history. The center's exhibits will whet your appetite for the trail ahead, which includes fine views from Ball Mountain and a visit to two of New Jersey's most interesting old iron mines, the historic Roomy and Blue Mines.

Distance: 4.2-mile lollipop
Approximate hiking time: 3 hours
Difficulty/elevation gain: Moderate with a few good climbs
Trail surface: Rocky forest trails and old mine roads
Best seasons: Spring through fall
Other trail users: None
Canine compatibility: No dogs permitted at Weis Ecology Center; otherwise leashed dogs okay
Permits and fees: None
Schedule: Dawn to dusk

Maps: *DeLorme New Jersey Atlas & Gazetteer,* p. 25; *USGS Wanaque, NJ,* quadrangle; *North Jersey Trails Map #115*
Trail contacts: Ringwood State Park, 1304 Sloatsburg Rd., Ringwood, NJ 07456-1799; www .state.nj.us/dep/parksand forests/parks/norvin.html
Special considerations: Roomy Mine closed in winter for hibernating bats. May close more often due to bat disease.
Other: Be sure to visit the Weis Ecology Center.

Finding the trailhead: From the intersection of NJ 23 and Echo Lake Road (Passaic County Road 695) in Newfoundland, go northeast on Echo Lake Road. At the T intersection turn left onto Macopin Road, passing West Milford High School on the right. After driving 1.5 miles turn right (east) onto Westbrook Road and travel 5.0 miles. Turn right (north) onto Snake Den Road (East). (*Warning:* You will pass another Snake Den Road, but these roads are no longer connected.) At 0.3 mile bear left (south) at the fork, staying with Snake Den Road. At 0.6 mile Weis Ecology Center's parking lot is on the right. **GPS:** N41° 04.18' / W74° 19.34'

The Hike

The New Jersey Audubon's Weis Ecology Center, our starting point, is worth a visit and has an interesting history. It started in 1921 as Camp Midvale, operated by the Nature Friends (originally *Naturfreunde,* of German origin). This politically liberal, social democratic organization provided working–class members with access to the outdoors. It attracted a variety of leftist artists, actors, and other notables over the years. In the 1950s McCarthy era, it was even scrutinized by the FBI, but its activities were always found to be proper. By 1974 it was in financial decline, and the property was sold to Walter and May Weis, who had it permanently protected and set up as an environmental center. In 1994 it became an official New Jersey Audubon Society Center. Check it out.

The Roomy Mine (probably named after a local family, originally spelled Roome) was also known as the Laurel or the Red Mine, and it operated from 1840 to 1857. With a flashlight, some protective headgear (or a hard head), and good boots, you can crawl through the opening and into a horizontal shaft cut 100 feet into the solid rock of the mountain. The only hazards you'll face are mud and the occasional bat (harmless). Drilled holes visible in the rock testify to the hard work of mining by hammer, drill, and blasting powder. (*Note:* The mine is closed [it's the law] between September 1 and April 30, while the bats hibernate. It may be closed more often because of a fungus affecting the bats.)

The nearby Blue Mine (a.k.a. the London, Iron Hill, or

Whynockie Mine) is much older, having been opened by German iron entrepreneur Peter Hasenclever in 1765. It operated intermittently until 1905, when it closed for good. But unlike the Roomy Mine, the Blue Mine is little more today than a great flooded hole in the ground.

This hike may get you to thinking: Is it Wyanokie, Wanaque, Whynockie, or what? The original Native American Lenape name for the region was something like "Wah-*nah*-kay" or "Why-hah-*nah*-key." As with so many native words, there are variant opinions on its meaning: "rest and repose," says one source; "place of sassafras," say a number of others. It appears the first European to write down the name was a Frenchman, who rendered it phonetically in French: "Wa-na-ke." Ever after, the name has frequently been pronounced "Wan*na*-cue," even though old-timers will insist it's "Wa-*na*-key." And there are myriad other spellings: Wynokie, Wynocky, Wynoky, Wynockie, Whinockie. . . .

Miles and Directions

0.0 From the Weis Ecology Center parking lot, walk to the west end of the lot and locate the New Jersey Audubon Society's kiosk. Just beyond the sign and up the paved lane, the Otter-Hole trailhead (green blaze) is found. Within 100 yards the trail turns left (west) off the lane and crosses the lawn and under a canopy of Norway spruce.

0.1 Pass the L Trail coming in on the left (south), which becomes co-aligned with the Otter-Hole Trail. The route parallels the Blue Mine Brook and the picnic tables, and it skirts the natural pool.

0.2 Turn left (south) onto a trail, following the green blazes of the Otter-Hole Trail and leaving the woods road and L Trail. The route meanders along the Blue Mine Brook and above the natural pool.

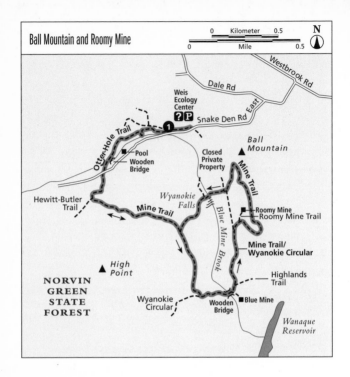

Ball Mountain and Roomy Mine

0 Kilometer 0.5

0 Mile 0.5

N

Westbrook Rd

Dale Rd

Weis Ecology Center

? P

Snake Den Rd

East

Ball ▲ Mountain

Closed Private Property

Mine Trail

Otter-Hole Trail

Pool

Wooden Bridge

Wyanokie Falls

Roomy Mine
Roomy Mine Trail

Hewitt-Butler Trail

Mine Trail

Blue Mine Brook

Mine Trail/ Wyanokie Circular

High Point ▲

Highlands Trail

NORVIN GREEN STATE FOREST

Wyanokie Circular

Wooden Bridge

■ Blue Mine

Wanaque Reservoir

0.3 Turn left (south) and cross the wooden bridge.

0.4 Cross Snake Den Road onto the Mine Trail (yellow on white blaze) and the Hewitt-Butler Trail (blue blaze), which are co-aligned. The trail rises up through the rocks. (**FYI:** The Otter-Hole Trail turns right up the road.)

0.5 At the trail junction turn left (south), remaining with the Mine Trail (yellow on white). (**FYI:** The Hewitt-Butler Trail continues straight [west].)

0.9 Pass on the left (east) the other end of the Mine Trail. (**FYI:** This is your return route.)

1.2 At the trail junction the Mine Trail (yellow on white) contin- ues straight (south) onto a woods road, which is co-aligned with Wyanokie Circular (red blaze) and the Highlands Trail. Shortly the route turns left off the woods road and onto a trail. (**FYI:** The Wyanokie Circular and the Highlands Trail also proceed right [west].)

1.4 Cross over Blue Mine Brook via a wooden bridge. The Mine Trail turns left (north) and onto a mine road. (**Side trip:** To visit the Blue Mine, turn right and travel 90 feet to view the gaping maw of its shaft.) (**FYI:** The Highlands Trail departs right [east] within 35 feet.)

1.6 Turn right (northeast) off the mine road and onto a trail, all the while following the Mine Trail and the yellow-on-white blazes.

1.7 After the first rise onto a shelf, there is a trail junction with the Roomy Mine Trail (orange blaze). The Mine Trail continues straight and continues to climb. (**Side trip:** To visit the Roomy Mine, turn left, following the orange blazes for about 40 feet.)

1.9 Reach the top of the ridge, bear left, and follow its contour, crossing a series of peaks, spoil piles (mining waste rock), and bedrock.

2.3 Arrive at Ball Mountain, with its impressive western view. Take note of how the glacier polished the bedrock. Descend (southwest) off the ridge on the trail.

2.4 At the intersection with the Wyanokie Circular Trail (red), continue straight (west), remaining on the Mine Trail.

2.6 Arrive at Wyanokie Falls and rock hop across Blue Mine Brook.

2.9 At the T intersection turn right (north) and retrace the Mine Trail back to the parking lot.

4.2 Arrive back at the parking lot.

2 Monks Mountain

A noble little loop hike that takes you to the peak of Monks Mountain, sharing several views from the top, where you will look down on Monksville Reservoir. Explore (carefully) the prickly pear cactus found bordering one of the vistas. The route also takes you by the nineteenth-century Monks, or Winston, Mine, with its gaping maw. Locating magnetite ore with a magnet might be a fun break from the hike.

Distance: 2.7-mile loop

Approximate hiking time: A leisurely 2 hours

Difficulty/elevation gain: Easy, with the exception of 1 challenging climb

Trail surface: Rocky forest trails and mine roads

Best seasons: All

Other trail users: None

Canine compatibility: Leashed dogs permitted

Permits and fees: None

Schedule: Dawn to dusk

Maps: New York–New Jersey Trail Conference *North Jersey Trails Map #115*; *DeLorme New Jersey Atlas & Gazetteer*, p. 20; *USGS Greenwood Lake, NJ*, quadrangle

Trail contacts: Ringwood State Park, 1304 Sloatsburg Rd., Ringwood, NJ 07456-1799; www .state.nj.us/dep/parksand forests/parks/norvin.html

Other: Another good hike in this area is the Sterling Ridge Trail at nearby Long Pond Ironworks Historic Site.

Finding the trailhead: From NJ 23 in Newfoundland, take Union Valley Road north for 7.2 miles. At a fork turn right on Marshall Hill Road for 1.5 miles. Turn right onto Greenwood Lake Turnpike for approximately 3 miles, passing Long Pond Ironworks Historic Site and crossing the causeway over Monksville Reservoir. At the end of the causeway, turn right and enter the parking lot. The trail is at the southwest end of the parking lot. **GPS:** N41° 08.18' / W74° 18.46'

The Hike

The quote opening this guide is from the book *Winbeam,* Minnie Mae Monks's 1930 elegy to the nature, people, and landscape of the Wanaque Valley, much of it already lost under the Wanaque Reservoir by the time the book was published. The Monks family gave its name to Monksville, which itself was swept away. The charm of the old Wanaque Valley is lost forever, but much natural beauty remains in the area.

Following the severe drought of the 1960s, the North Jersey District Water Supply Commission examined ways to augment the storage capacity of Wanaque Reservoir. The result was a plan for a new reservoir upstream from the Wanaque: Monksville Reservoir. After two decades of planning and construction by the Wanaque South Project, this artificial lake was completed in 1987.

Although these two reservoirs swallowed up the villages of Boardville and Monksville, the historic iron-making hamlet of Hewitt survived. Better known today as Long Pond Ironworks, this State and National Historic Site includes homes, stores, and industrial ruins from the 1760s through the 1920s. A hike up the nearby Sterling Ridge Trail will take you past the village and furnace ruins, up to a grand view of Greenwood Lake.

One of the places the Long Pond iron furnaces likely got ore is the Monks (Winston) Mine, whose impressive remains are a highlight of our hike. Large open pits, trenches, and shafts give a vivid view of the hard work that went into extracting ore from the earth. (*Caution:* The mine site is fascinating but potentially dangerous. Explore carefully!) For such a big operation, hard data about the mine is scarce. Also known as (possibly) the Vincent Mine, it operated from the mid-1860s until about 1890, when it was abandoned.

Prickly pear cactus (PPC), with its yellow-orange flowers and red-purple fruit, adorns the top vistas from June to August. It can grow upright or like a carpet, as it does here. Also called "no pal," or "devil's tongue," this is the only native cactus found in the Garden State. It appreciates dry, sandy, or rocky soil where it is hot and sunny. Besides Monks Mountain, PPC grows on Mount Tammany's peak (Delaware Water Gap), along the Jersey Shore, and throughout the Pine Barrens. In some parts of our country, PPC is cultivated and sold commercially. The peeled fruit has varied uses: juices and jellies, puree and pickles, soups and salads, teas and candy. Seeds may be roasted and pads cooked as a vegetable. It has been made into an intoxicant beverage and at the same time used to cure hangovers. The Native Americans would place the PPC juices on burns. There also appears to be medical interest in PPC for various conditions. Overall, it's an amazing plant. Of course, it's absolutely prohibited to take any part of the cactus. Besides—*Warning!*—the PPC barbed bristles can inflict sharp pain.

Miles and Directions

0.0 The Monks Trail (white blaze) is located at the west end of the parking lot. Circumvent the auto gate onto a gravel road and immediately bear right (west-southwest) onto a trail, paralleling the Monksville Reservoir.

0.3 Turn left (east) onto the pipeline and immediately cross the gravel road diagonally (south) onto an ascending trail.

0.5 Cross under power lines and onto a woods road.

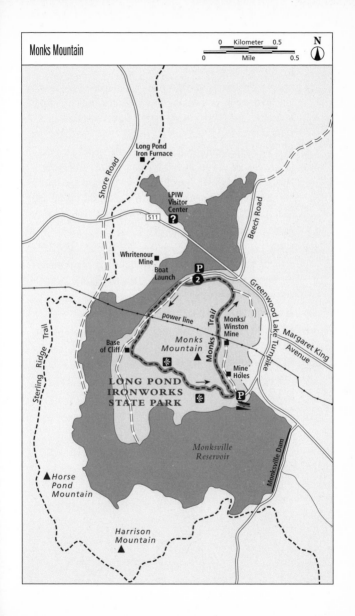

Monks Mountain

0.7 Arrive at the base of the cliffs.

0.9 Arrive at the top of an outcrop and unofficial outlook, found left of the trail. A nice lunch spot.

1.1 Arrive at the official side trail (blue blaze) leading to the right (south) 0.1 mile to a vista of Monksville Reservoir, Harrison Mountain, and Board Mountain. The Monks Trail continues straight (east).

1.6 After descending off the ridge on a woods road/trail, arrive at a trail junction and cross the stream. Within 44 feet the Monks Trail leaves left (west) off the woods road and onto a trail. It's easy to miss this turn. (**FYI:** Trails to the right [east] lead to the Monksville Dam parking lot.)

1.7 Pass on the right a series of mine holes.

1.9 At the T intersection with the mine road, turn left (north) onto the road. (**FYI:** The Monks [Winston] Mine is located 75 feet on the right [east] side of the lane. Please use caution near these open pits!)

2.3 At the Y intersection bear left, and within 100 yards turn left (west) again onto a trail and away from the sights and sounds of CR 511.

2.4 Pass a green-blazed trail on your right.

2.7 Turn right (east) onto a woods road, arriving back at the parking lot.

3 Lake Lookout

This out-and-back hike travels through hardwood forest: beeches, oaks, and maples. Pass through canyons of rhododendrons, mountain laurel, and hemlocks. Climb to the top of ridges edged by granite cliffs. Skirt a bog and swamp. All with the potential to observe wildlife: bear, deer, porcupine, and an array of birds. Arrive at secluded Lake Lookout, an ideal lunch spot.

Distance: 5.2-mile out-and-back

Approximate hiking time: 3 hours

Difficulty/elevation gain: Moderate, with some climbing

Trail surface: Old woods roads

Best seasons: All

Other trail users: Multiuse

Canine compatibility: Leashed dogs permitted

Permits and fees: None

Schedule: Dawn to dusk

Maps: New York–New Jersey Trail Conference *North Jersey Trails Map #116; DeLorme New Jersey Atlas & Gazetteer, p. 20; USGS Wawayanda, NJ,* quadrangle

Trail contacts: Wawayanda State Park, 885 Warwick Tpk., Hewitt, NJ 07421; (973) 853-4462; www.state.nj.us/dep/parksand forests/parks/wawayanda.html

Finding the trailhead: Follow NJ 23 9.6 miles north from its I-287 exit. Just north of Newfoundland, take the NJ 23 exit for LaRue Road and Clinton Road. Take Clinton Road north for 7.5 miles through watershed lands, with Clinton Reservoir on your left. *Caution:* There are some sharp bends in this road. The parking lot will be on your left. *Note:* The parking area is easy to miss. If you start seeing signs of civilization (like houses and lakes), you've gone too far. **GPS:** N41° 08.58' / W74° 24.45'

The Hike

This route passes glacial lakes in succession—namely swamps. After thousands of years the lakes gradually fill with earthen debris and eventually plant growth. Each year the water level fluctuates, rising during the winter snows and spring rains and evaporating during the summer. The succession appears like a painting: The foreground germinates skunk cabbage, ferns, and sedges; the middle ground grows spicebush, blueberry, and witch hazel; and in the background stand red maples, yellow birch, and eastern hemlocks. Upon viewing these swamps you could be fortunate enough to see a heron, a raptor, and a bear, all taking advantage of the changing environs.

The area we travel through was also the route of one of America's earliest pipelines. Although traces of it are scant now, the Olean-Bayonne oil pipeline once passed through here. Built in 1881 by John D. Rockefeller, it brought crude oil from Olean, New York, to the Bayonne, New Jersey, refineries. For a time Rockefeller's firm, Standard Oil, actually owned some 6,000 acres here, but they later sold it. The Olean-Bayonne pipeline stopped pumping crude in 1927 but was later retrofitted to pump natural gas. It was supplanted in 1955 by a new and even bigger pipeline, which likewise cuts through the park here: the Tennessee natural gas pipeline, now owned by the El Paso Corporation.

A feature of our walk is Lake Lookout, built by Fred Ferber, an Austrian who immigrated to the United States in 1932 and made a fortune in ballpoint pen patents and manufacture. For some forty-plus years, from 1918 until the early 1960s, about 7,000 acres here were owned by the

New Jersey Zinc Company, which timbered it for mine props. When they decided to sell the property around 1960, both Ferber and the state of New Jersey wanted to purchase the land. They finally split it, with New Jersey buying 4,000 acres around Lake Wawayanda and Ferber getting the remaining 3,000 acres.

Ferber was a progressive thinker and an ardent devotee of nature—he operated his property as a wildlife preserve, permitting access to school groups and educators. He kept this natural land here from 1960 until 1973, when he encountered financial difficulties. In the end he sold it at cost to the state of New Jersey for Wawayanda State Park.

Miles and Directions

0.0 From the parking lot turn right (west) onto the shoulder of Clinton Road and travel 200 feet. Turn right (northwest) again and proceed around the Project U.S.E. gate where the Old Coal Trail (red blaze) begins as a gravel lane. The trail cuts through the camp.

0.4 At the fork bear right, staying with the Old Coal Trail (red) where the woods road begins to climb. (**FYI:** The trail bearing left is the Bearfort Waters/Clinton Trail [yellow blaze].)

0.5 Continue straight (north) on the woods road, ignoring the unmarked woods road to the right.

0.8 Pass through an area beautifully stitched by stone fences.

1.5 Along the top of the ridge, continue straight on Old Coal Trail, passing Turkey Ridge Trail (green blaze) on your left (west).

1.7 Just prior to crossing the El Paso/Tennessee natural gas pipeline clearing, you cross the route of the historic Olean-Bayonne oil pipeline. If you miss it, you can check it out on the return trip. Remain on the woods road.

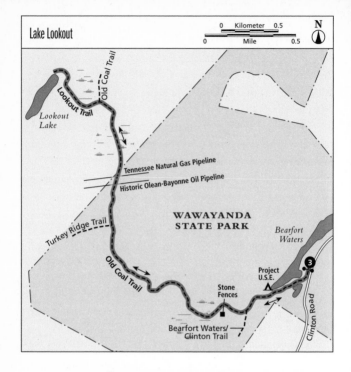

Lake Lookout

Lookout Lake

Lookout Trail

Old Coal Trail

Tennessee Natural Gas Pipeline

Historic Olean-Bayonne Oil Pipeline

WAWAYANDA
STATE PARK

Bearfort
Waters

Turkey Ridge Trail

Old Coal Trail

Project
U.S.E.

Stone
Fences

Clinton Road

Bearfort Waters/
Clinton Trail

1.8 Tramp through 200 yards of potentially damp muck while skirting the swamp.

2.3 Arrive at a trail junction under a canopy of large white pines. Turn left (west) onto Lookout Trail (white blazes), a woods road, leaving Old Coal Trail to continue straight.

2.6 Edge around the north end of Lake Lookout, crossing over the outlet, and arrive at the ledges above the lake. This is your turnaround spot; retrace the route.

5.2 Arrive back at the Clinton Road parking lot.

4 Governor Mountain

This lollipop outing epitomizes the "best easy hikes" concept: a gentle ascent through hardwood forest up to a peak of eastern red cedars, moss, and glacial erratics strewn about like children's oversize blocks. From the ledges you find a beautiful western view of the mountains (Board, Bear, and Windbeam) and the Wanaque Reservoir. There's one short steep descent; otherwise the footing is relatively easy.

Distance: 2.4-mile loop

Approximate hiking time: 2 hours

Difficulty/elevation gain: Easy, with moderate climbs

Trail surface: Forest path

Best seasons: All

Other trail users: Multiuse

Canine compatibility: Dogs allowed

Permits and fees: None

Schedule: Dawn to dusk

Maps: New York–New Jersey Trail Conference *North Jersey Trails Map #115*; USGS *Wanaque, NJ* quadrangle; *DeLorme New Jersey Atlas & Gazetteer*, p. 26

Trail contacts: Ringwood State Park, 1304 Sloatsburg Rd., Ringwood, NJ 07456-1799; www .state.nj.us/dep/parksand forests/parks/norvin.html

Finding the trailhead: From I-287, take exit 57 for Skyline Drive and Ringwood. Follow Skyline Drive for 4.8 miles to its end, turning right onto Greenwood Lake Turnpike. Follow this for 0.8 mile, turning right onto Skylands Road. Follow this for another 0.8 mile into the community of Cupsaw Lake. Turn left at Cupsaw Avenue for 200 feet, then turn left again onto Cupsaw Drive, which shortly becomes Carletondale Road. Follow this for 0.7 mile to the Community Presbyterian Church. Ask for permission to park in their lot. **GPS:** N41° 07.13' / W74° 15.59'

The Hike

For most of American history, a very different view greeted you here. Wanaque Reservoir is a product of the 1920s; before that you saw spread before you the Wanaque Valley, a fertile farm valley with the little hamlets of Boardville and Monksville and the New York & Greenwood Lake Railroad chugging its way up the valley. It was, in the words of one nineteenth-century historian, "one of the most picturesque and beautiful valleys in the state." No more.

The name Boardville reflects the influence of pioneer Cornelius Board, a Welsh émigré who came to America to operate mines and ironworks. He settled in this area around 1737, starting ironworks at Stirling and Ringwood (where the little Board Homestead still stands). This pioneering iron industrialist sold his ironworks around 1740 and settled at Boardville, at the confluence of the Wanaque River and Ringwood Creek. His son, Colonel Joseph Board, built a handsome stone farmhouse there, just one of the centuries-old landmarks that was destroyed when the reservoir was built. The Board family cemetery, along with three others, was dug up and moved in 1922 in preparation for the new reservoir.

So which "Governor" was this mountain named after? None. According to Ralph Colfax, president of the North Jersey Highlands Historical Society, the mountain was named after Nicholas Gouverneur, a business partner with the Ogden family in the Ringwood Ironworks in the 1750s. The name probably dates to the late 1800s era of the Hewitts of Ringwood Manor, who liked historical names and applied them liberally to these hills near their country estate (they owned most of the hills, after all). Aside from his role in the early iron industry here, Nicholas Gouverneur is most famous for his nephew, Gouverneur Morris, the Colonial statesman who was a representative to the Constitutional Convention of 1787, and in that capacity wrote these rather famous words for the Preamble of that document: "We the People of the United States, in Order to form a more perfect Union . . . "

Miles and Directions

0.0 Exit the Community Presbyterian Church (C.P.C.) parking lot and turn left (north) onto the shoulder of Carletondale Road. (**Option:** While gaining permission to park at the C.P.C, gain dispensation to enter the Cooper Union Trail [C.U.T.] at the west end of their lot via a 30-foot-long trail. Turn left [north] onto the C.U.T. [mile 0.3 on the route]. The church uses this shortcut for Sunday services on Governor Mountain from June through August [7 a.m.].)

0.1 Arrive at the Cooper Union Trail, which crosses Carletondale Road, and turn left (west) onto the trail, following yellow blazes.

0.3 Prior to a wooden bridge, pass an unofficial trail to the left (east) leading to the church parking lot.

0.4 At the intersection continue straight (southwest). (**FYI:** The hike will return via the trail to the left, so make a mental note of this spot.)

1.0 Pass over the summit with its scattered glacial erratics and stand of eastern red cedar.

1.1 Pass by an illegal fire ring and shortly arrive at a ledge with a clear view of the Wanaque Reservoir, Board Mountain, Bear Mountain, and Windbeam Mountain. The trail descends from the left (south) side of the vistas and shortly edges the ridge, heading east. (**FYI:** One hundred yards from the top, the former trail leads [west] 150 feet to Suicide Ledge, a must-see.)

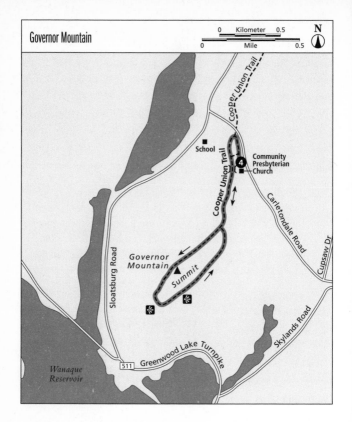

Governor Mountain

0 Kilometer 0.5
0 Mile 0.5

N

School

Cooper Union Trail

Community
Presbyterian
Church

4

Cooper Union Trail

Carletondale Road

Cupsaw Dr

Governor
Mountain

▲ Summit

Sloatsburg Road

Skylands Road

Greenwood Lake Turnpike

511

Wanaque
Reservoir

- **1.2** Climb down a short steep section.
- **1.3** Pass an outcropping on the right (south), begging to be explored.
- **1.9** Descend (north) off the ridge, leaving the bedrock and glacial erratics.
- **2.0** At the T intersection turn right (northeast) and retrace your steps.
- **2.4** Arrive back at the parking lot.

5 Ramapo Lake and Castle Point

This rather challenging hike packs a lot into a loop. Tramp past the photogenic ruins of Van Slyke Castle and the stone water tower. Edge Ramapo Lake and climb Castle Point. View the New York City skyline as well as the Watchung Mountains and the Wyanokie Plateau. There are two steady rises on this hike, but it's well worth the effort.

Distance: 2.9-mile loop

Approximate hiking time: 3 hours

Difficulty/elevation gain: Easy, with 2 steep, challenging climbs

Trail surface: Rocky trails and old woods roads

Best seasons: Spring through fall

Other trail users: Multiuse

Canine compatibility: Dogs allowed

Permits and fees: None

Schedule: Dawn to dusk

Maps: New York–New Jersey Trail Conference *North Jersey Trails Map #116; DeLorme New Jersey Atlas & Gazetteer, p. 26; USGS Wanaque, NJ,* quadrangle

Trail contacts: Ringwood State Park, 1304 Sloatsburg Rd., Ringwood, NJ 07456-1799; www .state.nj.us/dep/parksand forests/parks/norvin.html

Finding the trailhead: From I-287 west of Oakland, take exit 57 for Ringwood/Skyline Drive. Get on Skyline Drive north and take it for 1.2 miles to the top of the mountain. The trailhead and parking lot are on the left. *Note:* You will pass a different trailhead parking lot closer to the bottom of Skyline Drive on the left; don't confuse it with the one you need, which is farther up the mountain. **GPS:** N41° 02.85' / W74° 15.09'

The Hike

Our hike in the Ramapos begins on Skyline Drive and ambles down a rocky, old woods road, the Hoeferlin Memorial Trail. Bill Hoeferlin was a pioneering North Jersey trail builder and mapmaker; thus the honor of having the trail named after him is deserved. Reaching Ramapo Lake near its spillway, we follow an old road along the shore. The lake was originally called Rotten Pond, a term not pejorative but descriptive, likely a corruption of the early Dutch settlers' word "rot," meaning rat (i.e., muskrat), which presumably flourished in its waters. The road is the MacEvoy Trail, named for Clifford E. MacEvoy, the construction magnate (builder of Wanaque Reservoir) who owned this property. MacEvoy's estate, including a unique observatory tower, survives above the lakeshore here (private). The remainder of his land was bought by the state of New Jersey in 1976, becoming Ramapo Mountain State Forest.

The trail shortly heads back up the mountain along the Castle Point Trail, a rigorous climb that rewards hikers with views of the New York City skyline and a romantic ruin at the top. Its story begins around 1907 with the elderly Charles E. Halliwell, a partner in the American Tobacco Company. He had recently married his pretty young nurse, Alice Cole. Alice Halliwell was left a widow a year later, and in short order married William Porter. Porter was a partner of Halliwell's in the American Tobacco Company, and thus in the same league as nicotine millionaires Pierre Lorillard of Tuxedo Park and James Buchanan Duke of Hillsborough, New Jersey.

The "castle" whose shell gives this trail its name was really a stone mansion called Foxcroft built by William and Alice Porter in 1909, soon after their marriage. Foxcroft was built as their summer home, but it enjoyed brief bliss: Porter was killed in a car crash in 1911, leaving Alice Cole Halliwell Porter a widow for the second time.

Mrs. Porter soon married Warren C. Van Slyke, who survived a surprising (for her) twelve years, dying in 1925. Mrs. Alice C. H. P. Van Slyke thereafter resided in Foxcroft alone until she joined her three husbands in death in 1940. In the years that followed, the mansion was embroiled in a nasty divorce and lawsuit, sat empty for years, and finally burned down in 1959, becoming the sad ruin you see today. (*Explore with caution!* You could get hurt here.) It may have the atmosphere of a medieval ruin or a dark gothic fantasy, but it's just a sad relic of a family with an unhappy history.

Farther up we visit the equally interesting stone water tower that served the estate, another reminder of the days when wealth called the Ramapo Mountains its playground.

Miles and Directions

0.0 Head to the back of the parking lot, where numerous paths lead to the Hoeferlin Memorial Trail (yellow blaze), which parallels the back lot. Turn left (south) on the trail. Shortly, you'll pass a kiosk on the left and a trailhead sign for the Hoeferlin and begin to head west.

0.1 The trail heads south diagonally across another gravel road, eventually descending.

0.2 Cross over a culvert/stream and within 100 yards turn left (south) onto a trail, leaving the gravel road. The trail runs along the ridge, with views of the cliff and the hollow.

0.3 At the T intersection turn right (north) onto a woods road and, shortly, onto the MacEvoy Trail (blue blaze). The road shortly becomes a trail. (**FYI:** The Hoeferlin and MacEvoy Trails are co-aligned.)

1.0 At the T intersection turn left onto a gravel auto road and within 30 yards veer right (north), remaining with the Mac-Evoy Trail (blue blaze). The trail borders Ramapo Lake on a

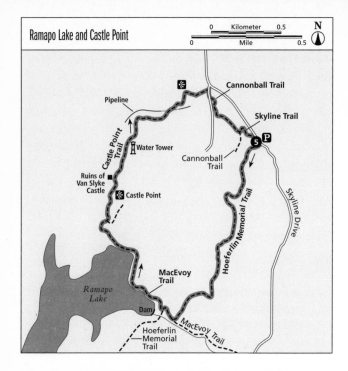

Ramapo Lake and Castle Point

Cannonball Trail

Skyline Trail

Pipeline

Castle Point Trail

Water Tower

Cannonball Trail

Ruins of Van Slyke Castle

Castle Point

Hoeferlin Memorial Trail

Skyline Drive

MacEvoy Trail

Ramapo Lake

Dam

Hoeferlin Memorial Trail

MacEvoy Trail

one-lane road. (**Side trip:** To visit the dam, veer left on the Hoeferlin Trail, which runs along the top of the dam.)

1.5 At the Y intersection bear right (north) onto a one-lane road, where the MacEvoy Trail begins to ascend.

1.6 Turn left (west) onto the Castle Point Trail (white blaze), which is a gravel road. Within 170 feet look for signage for Castle Point Trail. Turn left (north) onto a trail and begin a steep ascent.

1.7 Arrive at Castle Point, a series of rock outcrops with inspiring views and a place to rest.

1.8 Arrive at the ruins of Van Slyke Castle, where the route edges the stone walls and travels under the steel beams. As the trail moves away from the burned-out structure, it runs northeast along the ridge.

2.0 Pass the monolithic water tower.

2.2 The trail drops off the ridge, eventually veering right (southeast) under the power lines, where it shortly turns right onto a woods road.

2.3 At the junction with a pipeline, turn right (east) where the trail is co-aligned with the pipeline.

2.4 Just before the pipeline path rises, turn right (east) onto a rocky trail and begin a short, steep, steady climb to the last vista on the hike.

2.5 Turn right (south) onto a paved road and in 100 yards turn left (east) onto the Cannonball Trail (red blaze).

2.6 At the Y intersection bear left (southeast) onto Skyline Trail (red/white blaze).

2.9 Arrive back at the parking lot.

6 Tripod Rock

This extraordinary jaunt takes you through Pyramid Mountain Natural Historical Area's natural sculpture garden. We pass amazing erratics: Bear Rock, possibly New Jersey's largest, and Tripod Rock, a balanced pedestal rock claimed by some to have links to the solstice and prehistoric sun worship. Along with views of the Newark Basin and the New York City skyline, there are side trips to the Morgan Place foundations, Cole Farm Mine, and Lucy's Overlook.

Distance: 5.0-mile lollipop
Approximate hiking time: 2.5 hours
Difficulty/elevation gain: Moderate, with a few rocky stretches
Trail surface: Rocky trails and woods roads
Best seasons: All
Other trail users: None
Canine compatibility: Leashed dogs permitted
Permits and fees: None
Schedule: Dawn to dusk
Maps: *DeLorme New Jersey Atlas & Gazetteer,* p. 25; *USGS Boonton and Pompton Plains,*
NJ, quadrangles; a Morris County Park Commission map is available at the site and on their Web site (http://parks.morris.nj.us)
Trail contacts: Morris County Park Commission, 53 E. Hanover Ave., P.O. Box 1295, Morristown, NJ 07962-1295; (973) 326-7600; info@parks.morris.nj.us; http://parks.morris.nj.us; Pyramid Mountain Visitor Center, (973) 334-3130
Special considerations: This park is likely to be crowded on nice weekends.

Finding the trailhead: From the intersection of NJ 23 northbound and Boonton Avenue, take the U-turn for Boonton Avenue (Morris County Road 511). Turn right onto Boonton Avenue (MCR 511) and proceed 4.2 miles. Turn right (west) into the Pyramid Mountain Natural Historical Area parking lot. **GPS:** N40° 56.74' / W74° 23.36'

The Hike

The outstanding features of this hike are Bear Rock and Tripod Rock, must-sees on any visit here. Both are amazing but in different ways. Any way you look at it, a hike here is like a hike through a geological sculpture garden.

Bear Rock is alleged to be the largest boulder in New Jersey. Known early on as "Bare" rock, some say it looks like a bear, or perhaps it was bare. Whatever the case, Native Americans found a use for this colossal rock next to a stream and a swamp. Ancient rock shelters existed on both sides of it, used as transient camps by hunting and foraging parties.

Tripod Rock has a different story. As you will see when visiting the site, it is a 160-something-ton boulder, roughly triangular, balanced at an angle on three smaller boulders, at a height of some 2 feet. Looking like a precarious joke left by an ancient race of giants, it is one of the great wonders of New Jersey. A geological wonder, most would say—the last ice age deposited untold glacial erratics across the mountains of northern New Jersey. It stands to reason that some of them would end up in unusual configurations. Tripod Rock is a monument to the power (albeit random) of natural geological forces.

Pshaw, says another camp. How can anything so obviously artificial be dismissed as a work of nature? Over the past several decades, some researchers have advanced a belief that North America is filled with ancient, huge rock monuments—megaliths—placed by ancient cultures to mark important dates in the calendar such as a summer or winter solstice or a spring or fall equinox. Three boulders near Tripod Rock form a triangle that points (kinda, sorta) to the summer solstice. It is a calendar stone, an ancient astrological site, indeed, a spiritual energy vortex, they say.

The difference of opinion will surely continue. Every year in June, Tripod Rock is a busy place to be for the summer solstice. Some come to enjoy the beauty of the scene, some come to ponder the mysteries of geology and ancient civilizations, and some are probably waiting for a call from the Mother Ship. Any way you look at it, Tripod Rock is a good place to ponder the imponderables.

Miles and Directions

0.0   Proceed to the kiosk found on the northwest side of the parking lot. The Blue Trail (blue blaze), also known as the Mennen Trail and the Butler-Montville Trail, begins directly behind the kiosk, heading north through the hardwoods.

0.1   Cross Stony Brook via a wooden bridge.

0.2   At the fork with the Yellow Trail, continue on the Blue Trail by bearing left (northwest) and begin to ascend, crossing under the power lines.

0.4   Pass the White Trail (white blaze) on the left (west) and continue to climb, paralleling the power lines.

0.5   After cresting the shoulder of the ridge, continue straight (northwest) onto the Red Trail South (red blaze), leaving the Blue Trail, which turns right (north). (*Note:* The hike will return via the Blue Trail, so make a mental note of this spot.)

0.8   The trail passes through the bottomland and is a bit tricky to follow. Pay attention to the blazing.

1.0   Cross Bearhouse Brook via the bridge and immediately come to a T intersection. Turn right (north) onto the White Trail, a woods road, which rises above the bottomland and along some serious outcrops. (**Side trip:** At the T intersection turn left onto the White Trail and travel 200 feet to see the Mor-

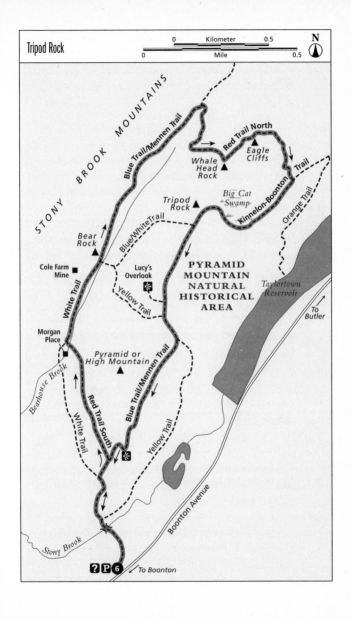

gan Place foundations. Supposedly during the late 1800s, the Morgans [Boonton bad boys] used it as a hideout.)

1.3 Arrive at a trail junction. Continue straight (north) on the woods road, passing Bear Rock on the left side, onto the Blue Trail, which comes in from the right (east). (**Option:** You can create a shorter loop to Tripod Rock and back to the visitor center by turning right [east] onto the co-aligned Blue Trail and White Trail.) (**Side trip:** If you are in the mood for adventure, bushwhack to the Cole Farm Mine. From Bear Rock, cross back over the stream and head due west for approximately 0.2 mile, avoiding the sheer outcropping. Ed Lenik, a local archaeologist, calls it ". . . a keyhole-shaped exploratory trench . . ." Look for a mound of mine tailings.)

2.0 Turn right (east) onto a relocated Red/White Trail (red and white blaze), which snakes across the bottomland.

2.3 At the end of the relocation, emerge onto the Red Trail North and steeply ascend onto the ridge.

2.4 Just beyond the crest of the ridge, pass Whale Head Rock on the right (south). The great blue has a grin on its face.

2.6 The trail descends steeply off Eagle Cliffs and proceeds to cross a washboard of ridges.

2.9 At the T intersection the Red Trail North ends. Turn right (southwest) onto the White Trail (Kinnelon-Boonton Trail, white blaze), which will run the ridge before dropping down past Big Cat Swamp.

3.6 Arrive at Tripod Rock. Besides the glacial erratics, you may have a bit more company here, as it's a popular destination. There is also a nice view of the hollow (northwest) from this spot. The trail continues from the south side of Tripod Rock, crossing a stream on rocks.

3.7 At the trail junction proceed straight (southwest) onto the Blue Trail, leaving the White Trail, which was co-aligned with the Blue Trail, as it turns right (northwest) and heads for Bear Rock.

3.8 Pass on the right a trail (blue and white blaze) leading to Lucy's Overlook. (**Side trip:** The rocky 0.1-mile trail ends at a secluded view of the Highlands region.)

3.9 At the fork bear left (southeast), continuing on the Blue Trail, which is now co-aligned with the Yellow Trail. The Yellow Trail to the right (west) leads to Cat Rocks and Bear Rock.

4.0 Pass the Yellow Trail, leaving left (east). Continue (south) on the Blue Trail, ascending the ridge.

4.3 Pass a vista on the left (southeast) with an impressive view of Turkey Mountain, Newark Basin, and the New York City skyline. It is also here that the trail turns sharply right (west), descending over a series of outcrops via switchbacks.

4.5 At the T intersection turn left (southeast) onto the Blue Trail and retrace the route back to the parking lot and the visitor center.

5.0 Arrive back at the parking lot.

7 The Torne/Osio Rock

This moderately easy hike takes you through a cleft in the Ramapo Mountains filled with interesting geological formations. From there it goes out to Osio Rock and the Torne, promontories with great views of the Wanaque Reservoir, the eastern Highlands, and the New York City skyline. The return trip includes a stop at the unique stone "Living Room," complete with a fireplace and easy chairs for your comfort.

Distance: 2.3-mile lollipop
Approximate hiking time: 3 hours
Difficulty/elevation gain: Moderately easy, with some steep stretches and a rocky climb
Trail surface: Rocky trails
Best seasons: Spring through fall
Other trail users: Multiuse
Canine compatibility: Dogs allowed

Permits and fees: None
Schedule: Dawn to dusk
Maps: New York–New Jersey Trail Conference *North Jersey Trails Map #115; USGS Wanaque, NJ,* quadrangle; *DeLorme New Jersey Atlas & Gazetteer,* p. 25.
Trail contacts: Ringwood State Park, 1304 Sloatsburg Rd., Ringwood, NJ 07456-1799; www.state.nj.us/dep/parksand forests/parks/norvin.html

Finding the trailhead: From NJ 23 north, take I-287 North at Riverdale for 0.6 mile. Take exit 53 and follow signs for Paterson Hamburg Turnpike, which later becomes Main Street. Follow for 1.7 miles and then turn right onto Glenwild Avenue. Follow this for roughly 3 miles. Passing the first state park parking lot, the second lot will be on your right. **GPS:** N41° 02.80' / W74° 21.20'

The Hike

If you do much hiking in the New York–New Jersey region, you will notice that "torne" (also spelled tourne) is a somewhat commonplace name for a tall, prominent mountain with good views. There are "tornes" in Ramapo, Boonton, Popolopen, here in the Wanaque Highlands, and elsewhere. The origin of this semi-generic term is with the early Dutch settlers in the area, who likened these haystack-like mountains with good views to "toren," Dutch for "tower." Some were indeed used as strategic lookout points during the Revolutionary War, when bonfires were built atop them.

This and several other of our hikes occur in Norvin Green State Forest, named for Norvin Hewitt Green (1893–1955), part of the famous Cooper-Hewitt clan that resided at Ringwood Manor from the 1850s to the 1930s. His maternal grandfather was Peter Cooper, the great early inventor and industrialist. Cooper's daughter Sarah married Abram S. Hewitt, who was Cooper's business partner in the iron industry, and later mayor of New York City.

The Hewitts' daughter Amy married Dr. James O. Green at Ringwood in 1886. Green's father was a pioneer in the telegraph industry and organized several smaller telegraph concerns into the Western Union Telegraph Company in 1866.

James and Amy's son, Norvin H. Green, was born in 1893. He spent much time at Ringwood with his aunts and uncles, among them Erskine Hewitt, who deeded Ringwood Manor to the state of New Jersey in 1936. Norvin was involved with a wide variety of business enterprises, including IBM. After Erskine Hewitt's death Norvin Green donated the contents of Ringwood Manor to the state as well, including antique furnishings, paintings, and other collections, ensuring that it would forever be seen as richly and uniquely furnished as it was when the Hewitts occupied it. In later years Norvin Green donated over 600 acres of land adjacent to Ringwood State Park, including some of the land that would later bear his name, as a state forest.

We get a good view of Wanaque Reservoir here, which merits mentioning a few pertinent facts. The North Jersey District Water Supply Commission was established in 1916 to build the reservoir, which has a watershed of ninety-four square miles. Eighty homes and farms were destroyed and four cemeteries and a railroad moved to make way for it. Originally providing one hundred million gallons of water daily, the Ramapo River diversion and Monksville Reservoir have increased that capacity to over 200 million gallons per day. It provides drinking water to eighty-five cities, towns, and boroughs in six counties in northeast New Jersey and is the single largest source of drinking water in the state.

Miles and Directions

- **0.0** From the parking lot turn left (south) onto the shoulder of Otter Hole Road.
- **0.1** Turn right (southwest) at a blaze post (red) onto the Torne Trail (red blaze). Within 100 feet cross the Hewitt-Butler Trail and continue straight up a rocky draw.
- **0.6** After the crest of the gorge and a slight descent, arrive at the T intersection with Hewitt-Butler Trail (blue blaze) and turn left (southeast) onto the Hewitt-Butler's rocky treadway bordered by glacial erratics.
- **0.8** Arrive at the first outcrop with splendid views.

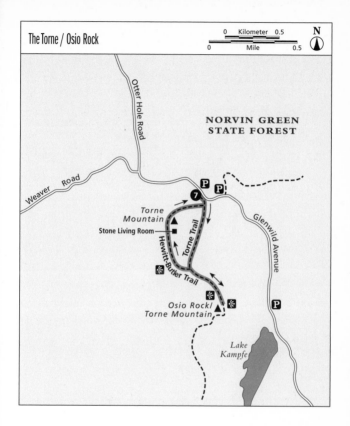

0   Kilometer   0.5

0   Mile   0.5

N

NORVIN GREEN
STATE FOREST

Otter Hole Road

Weaver Road

Glenwild Avenue

Torne
Mountain

Stone Living Room

Hewitt-Butler Trail

Torne Trail

Osio Rock/
Torne Mountain

Lake
Kampfe

1.0 Arrive at Osio Rock, also labeled Torne Mountain by the
USGS Greenwood Lake map (1910 edition), and the turnaround point. The peak has magnificent views of Mount
Warner (east), Carris Hill (northeast), High Point (northeast),
Assiniwikam Mountain (north), Wanaque Valley, East Highlands, and the Palisades. Retrace the route back to the trail
junction with Torne Trail (red).

1.4 At the junction with the Torne Trail, remain on the Hewitt-
Butler Trail (blue), crossing the draw and ascending steep

Torne Mountain. As you climb take your time and enjoy looking back off the bald escarpments and into the hollow. (**Bailout:** Retrace the Torne Trail back to the parking lot.)

1.9 Arrive at the peak of Torne Mountain, with its views west-northwest. Unofficial trails to the east lead to the stone Living Room, a scene from the 2500 B.C. stone circles found at Li Muri, Sardinia. Descend north off the peak, following blue blazing on tree trunks and on the bedrock.

2.2 At the intersection with the Torne Trail (red), turn left (north) onto the Torne and retrace the route back to the parking lot.

2.3 Arrive back at the parking lot.

The Piedmont

The Piedmont Province is a gently rolling plain that slopes from the foot of the rough Highlands southeast to the flat and sandy coastal plain. It contains less than a quarter of New Jersey's area. But because of its geology, with much good soil, and its geography, running between New York and Philadelphia, it has historically contained the bulk of New Jersey's population and development.

Mostly underlain with soft rocks—shale, siltstone, and sandstone—its undulating character is punctuated by dramatic cliffs and mountains, all of volcanic origin. In the north, diabase ridges form the famous Palisades of the Hudson, and to the south, the Sourland Mountains and others. Farther south the columnlike cliffs and mountains of the Watchung Range were formed by volcanic basalt forced upward like toothpaste out of innumerable tubes. Paterson's Garrett Mountain and the Great Falls are other reminders of this volcanic past.

At the end of the last ice age, some 10,000 years ago, the receding glacier left behind two great lakes near here as it melted. One of them, glacial Lake Passaic, survives as the vast wetlands of the Great Swamp. Another, glacial Lake Hackensack, is today the Hackensack Meadowlands.

The Piedmont contains some of the first land in New Jersey settled by Europeans. Its generally gentle terrain and rich soils encouraged farmers. By the colonial era they were producing copious quantities and varieties of fruits, vegetables, grains, dairy, livestock, and related products, including cider and spirits. One account credits British soldiers passing through this richly cultivated farmscape during the Revolution as saying that New Jersey was like one big garden—one possible origin of our nickname, the "Garden State."

With the waterpower available at places such as Paterson giving rise to an array of manufacturing enterprises, industry took root here, including ironworks, silk and textile mills, gun and locomotive works, and many others. Canals, such as the Morris Canal and the Delaware & Raritan Canal, aided this industry, as did later railroads.

In the twentieth century this region saw the greatest development and construction, with the corridor between New York and Philadelphia filling with highways and houses. As such, open space is precious in the Piedmont as nowhere else in New Jersey. Some of our earliest open spaces were established here, such as South Mountain and Watchung Reservations. These are green islands in a sea of industry and housing. The violence that 150 years of industrial activity did to the landscape is still visible in places, but fortunately recovery is under way, notably at places such as DeKorte Park in the Hackensack Meadowlands. All in all, the Piedmont is arguably the most "Jersey" part of New Jersey.

8 The Great Falls of the Passaic

Explore the birthplace of one of our nation's first planned industrial cities. This is an urban hike with sidewalks, street crossings, and paths. The route is a figure eight with spectacular views of the second-largest waterfall, by volume, east of the Mississippi River. As you stroll above and across the falls, the Passaic River plunges between sheer cliffs, creating rainbow mist over the scene. In contrast the Lower and Upper Raceways create a tranquil route.

Distance: 2.2-mile loop

Approximate hiking time: 2 hours

Difficulty/elevation gain: Easy

Trail surface: Sidewalks, paved trails, and gravel paths

Best seasons: All

Other trail users: You name it

Canine compatibility: Leashed dogs permitted

Permits and fees: None

Schedule: Dawn to dusk

Maps: *DeLorme New Jersey Atlas & Gazetteer,* p. 26; *USGS Paterson, NJ,* quadrangle; the most useful map is the one available at the Great Falls Visitors Center

Trail contacts: New Jersey Department of Environmental Protection, P.O. Box 402, Trenton, NJ 08625-0402; www .state.nj.us/dep. Great Falls Historic District Cultural Center, 65 McBride Ave. Extension, Paterson, NJ 07050; (973) 279-9587; greatfalls@patcity.org

Special considerations: In 2009 Congress designated the Great Falls of the Passaic a National Historic Site. What effect this will have on the site is unclear. Stay tuned. . . .

Other: Let it be noted: The maintaining agencies need to provide better stewardship of the resource. Meanwhile, be aware of your surroundings.

Finding the trailhead: Take I-80 to exit 57, toward downtown Paterson and Grand Street. Turn left on Grand Street or Avenue. Shortly turn right onto Spruce Street. After 3 blocks turn right onto McBride Avenue Extension. Overlook Park is located nearly opposite the Great Falls Visitors Center at 65 McBride Avenue Extension. **GPS:** N40° 54.93' / W74° 10.84'

The Hike

Although they're often called Paterson Falls, this seems decidedly unfair: The falls were known for a hundred years before the city of Paterson existed. Settlers in the 1600s noted their beauty, and 1700s picnic parties from as far away as New York came to see the massive waterfalls in the Jersey hinterlands. By volume, the only waterfall east of the Mississippi that's bigger is Niagara.

One such outdoor luncheon had enormous significance. In July 1778 two officers of the Continental Army took time off from fighting the British to enjoy some Madeira and provender whilst contemplating the thunderous foamy spray of the Great Falls. They were General George Washington and his aide-de-camp, Alexander Hamilton.

In 1791 Hamilton (now the first secretary of the U.S. Treasury) spearheaded the creation of a stock company to build a manufacturing city at the site. The Society for the Establishment of Useful Manufactures (S.U.M.) was founded via a stock offering and a government-sponsored lottery. New Jersey governor William Paterson gave his approval and assistance; in return the new city was named in his honor.

The S.U.M. acquired 700 acres around the Great Falls and set about building a three-tiered series of raceways to supply mill sites (the raceways are a notable part of our hike). As a manufacturing enterprise, the S.U.M. quickly stumbled and before long became merely the glorified land-lord of Paterson's waterpower resources.

There were ups and downs, but Paterson kept growing. Industrialist Peter Colt was among the first to operate in Paterson, making cotton cloth. In later years Paterson mills would produce something the Colt name is best known for: firearms. Paterson mills also made paper, machinery, locomotives, clothing, candles, soap, and chemicals. But its single most famous product was silk—for a generation, Paterson was known as Silk City.

In spite of this industrial growth, the Great Falls of the Passaic—no longer in the wilderness and greatly hemmed in by factories—remained a famous natural landmark. It was probably New Jersey's most famous scenic landmark in the 1800s, painted by landscape artists, extolled by poets, and admired by all.

Miles and Directions

0.0 Exit the entrance to Overlook Park and turn right (southwest) along McBride Avenue Extension, passing the Great Falls Historic District Cultural Center on the left.

0.1 At the fork bear right (northwest) along Spruce Street, passing the Great Falls and the S.U.M. Hydro-Electric Plant (built 1912-14).

0.2 At the intersection pass McBride Avenue and continue straight (northwest) onto Wayne Avenue, crossing over a bridge spanning the Passaic River with a view of the S.U.M. Dam (built 1838-40).

0.25 After passing Birch Street on the left, turn right (north) and proceed around the end of a cement wall, walk back (south-east) on a path toward the Passaic River, and immediately turn left (north), paralleling the riverbank. This earthen path-way has recently been cleared.

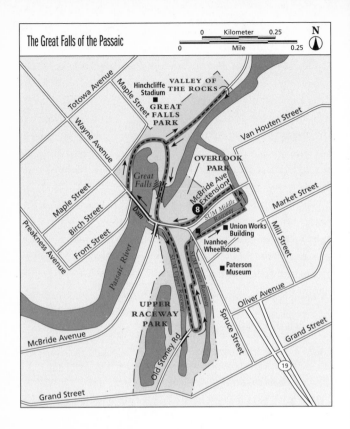

0.33 The trail merges with a macadam path coming in from the left (Maple Street) and continues straight (north) between two historic buildings: Steam and Boiler Plant (built 1876) on the left and Conduit Gate House (built 1906) on the right.

0.4 Turn right (southeast) after passing the Conduit Gate House and before the Hinchcliffe Stadium (built 1920). Pass the Pumping Station (built 1862) on the right.

0.45 At the fork before the Great Falls Park green, bear left (east), following the macadam bicycle path down the hill. (**Caution:** If you do not feel comfortable or safe here, skip and continue ahead.)

0.5 As you descend, pass a path on the right (southeast).

0.7 Arrive at the Valley of the Rocks. At the foot of the magnificent 130-foot cliffs (left) and Paterson Animal Shelter (right), turn around and retrace your steps back up to Great Falls Park.

0.9 As you ascend, pass a path on your left. (**Option:** Turn left [southeast] on the macadam path and climb down stairs leading to the Passaic River. Sadly, you might have to scramble over broken furniture and refuse, but the payoff is an impressive view of the basin at the foot of the falls. Retrace your route back up to the bicycle path and turn left [southwest].)

0.95 Reaching the top of the cliffs at Great Falls Park, take the far fork to the left (south) along the Passaic River and the Great Falls (right). (**Option:** Along the path and to the right, there is an opening in the wrought-iron fence where stairs lead you to a bird's-eye view of the very top of the Great Falls!)

1.1 Cross a footbridge directly over the Great Falls, with a primal view of the Passaic River plunging 80 feet through a 280-foot gorge. Shortly, cross a second footbridge and through a cinder parking lot till you reach the intersection of Spruce Street, Wayne Avenue, and McBride Avenue. Cross (south) Spruce Street and turn left (southeast) onto the sidewalk, paralleling the upper raceway.

1.2 At the junction of Spruce Street and McBride Avenue Extension, turn right (south) into Raceway Park onto a path that parallels the lower and upper raceways. (**Option:** To return to the trailhead, turn left [north], crossing Spruce Street onto McBride Avenue Extension, where Overlook Park will be immediately on your left [northwest].)

1.5   Before a footbridge over the upper raceway, turn left (north-east) onto a path following the curve of the spillway as it drops to the lower raceways. At this elbow in the path, there is a nice lookout of the raceway and the mills. The path now heads north.

1.6   Turn right (east) onto a footbridge crossing over the lower raceway. Immediately turn left (north) onto the path.

1.8   Turn right (east) on the path before the backside of the Ivan-hoe Wheelhouse (1865) and proceed alongside (north) the wheelhouse.

1.9   To cross (east) Spruce Street safely, turn right (south), walking a block to the intersection with Market Street. Turn left (south), crossing Spruce Street, and return to the opposite side of Spruce from where you started. Continue on the path, paralleling the middle raceway (built 1792–1802) on the left (north) and passing the Union Works Building (built 1890) on the right (south). (**Option:** If you would like to visit the Paterson Museum [Rogers Locomotive Erecting Shop, 1871], turn right [south] and proceed along the entrance.)

2.1   Turn left (north) on the path as it follows the raceway.

2.15 Cross McBride Avenue Extension and turn left (west) along its sidewalk. (**Option:** Continue north along the raceway till it dead-ends [200 yards]. From up here you can view the Colt Gun Mill [built 1836]. Retrace your steps on the path back to McBride Avenue Extension.) Turn right on the sidewalk.

2.2   Turn right (northwest) into Overlook Park and return back to where the loop began.

⑨ South Mountain and Rahway River

This trail shadows the Rahway River, climbing up through the bottomlands, reaching the 25-foot-high Hemlock Falls before looping back on a bridle path. The nearly level hike has one steep rise and a river crossing that is a rock hop. Observe a park designed by the Olmsted Brothers and built by the Civilian Conservation Corps. Don't miss the geological phenomenon called "turtlebacks," which is found en route.

Distance: 5.8-mile loop
Approximate hiking time: 3 hours
Difficulty/elevation gain: Easy, with one moderate climb and a river rock hop
Trail surface: Bridle paths, trails
Best seasons: All
Other trail users: Horses
Canine compatibility: Leashed dogs permitted
Permits and fees: None
Schedule: Dawn to dusk

Maps: *DeLorme New Jersey Atlas & Gazetteer,* p. 32; *USGS Roselle and Caldwell, NJ,* quadrangles; a map is also available at the park
Trail contacts: County of Essex Department of Recreation & Cultural Affairs, 115 Clifton Avenue, Newark, NJ 07104; (973) 268-3500; www.essex-countynj .org/p/index.php
Other: High water will make the river crossing difficult.

Finding the trailhead: From exit 50B (Maplewood, Millburn) off I-78, travel north on Vaux Hall Road for 0.7 mile. At the T intersection turn left (west) onto Millburn Avenue. Millburn Avenue jogs right in 0.6 mile and becomes Essex Street (past the Millburn railroad station). At 0.2 mile turn right (north) onto Lackawanna Place and go 0.1 mile to the T intersection with Glen Avenue. Turn right onto Glen Avenue and immediately turn left into the Locust Grove parking lot. **GPS:** N40° 43.66' / W74° 18.28'

The Hike

We hike through one of America's first parks on this walk. Essex County was a pioneer in creating parks in New Jersey, and one of its first was South Mountain Reservation. This spot in the Watchungs is historic: Washington Rock here was the site of a signal beacon (one of a series) that warned the Continental Army of British approach while they were encamped in Morristown. In later decades the branch of the Rahway River here was dammed and a variety of mills and power plants erected; the ruins of one forms an interesting feature of the park. But its wildness attracted attention among conservationists in the 1890s. The first park parcel here was bought in 1896, and land acquisition continued for over a decade.

At the same time, the Essex County Parks Department set about making plans for the reservation. While leaving it mostly natural, they wanted a series of romantic drives, paths, walks, and other features, all of which we use on our ramble. To design this they chose the best: Frederick Law Olmsted, designer of Central Park in New York City and many other notable American landscapes. Olmsted died before much could be done, but his sons' firm, the Olmsted Brothers, finished the plans in 1902. Reforesting the land was a priority, with over 3,000 rhododendrons planted in 1910 alone. The rest of the park design was built over time, the last significant work being done by the Civilian Conservation Corps in the 1930s. Hemlock Falls, a focal point in all these plans, is in many ways the grand finale and centerpiece of this hike, and worth a special visit.

Alas, some original park features (rustic shelters, bridges, and benches) have fallen to ruin and vanished, and much of the rest of the park is in varying stages of overgrowth and decay. Olmsted's Central Park once suffered the same fate but was reborn when the Central Park Conservancy was established to restore it to its original elegance. Thankfully, South Mountain Reservation is following the same route: The recently established South Mountain Conservancy is working hard to bring the reservation back to the elegance and charm of its glory days.

Turtlebacks are a notable part of the local nomenclature—to the extent that the local zoo took the name. "Turtleback" refers to a geological phenomenon in which basalt fractured, leaving cracks to fill with minerals. When erosion took place, the softer basalt wore away while the harder minerals did not. This left the minerals deposited within the cracks extending above the basalt surface, creating hexagonal patterns resembling a turtle's back.

Miles and Directions

0.0 From the northwest side of the Locust Grove Parking Area, locate the Rahway Trail (white blaze) trailhead and proceed onto the trail.

0.5 Arrive at Diamond Mill Pond and continue straight (north) on a trail paralleling the Rahway River. (**FYI:** The Rahway Trail (white blaze) and the River Trail [bridle path] crisscross, merge, and part more times than you can count. You'll want to take the white blazes out and the bridle path back.)

0.9 Arrive at the abandoned power plant and Campbell's Pond. At the trail junction turn left (northeast) onto the bridle path and in 55 feet turn left (north) back onto the trail (white blaze).

1.4 Arrive at Painter's Point, which can be reached by crossing a boardwalk over the dam.

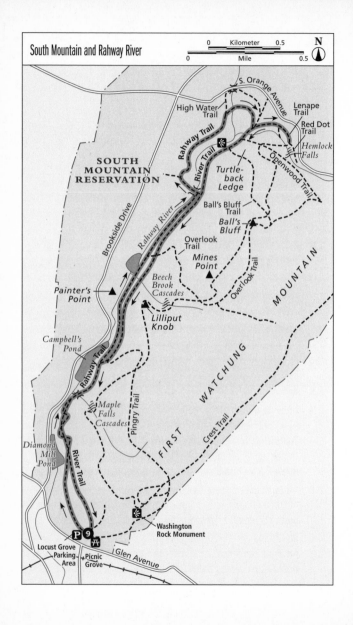

South Mountain and Rahway River

Kilometer
0   0.5

Mile
0   0.5

N

S. Orange Avenue

High Water Trail

Lenape Trail

Rahway Trail

River Trail

Red Dot Trail

Hemlock Falls

SOUTH MOUNTAIN RESERVATION

Turtle-back Ledge

Openwood Trail

Ball's Bluff Trail

Brookside Drive

Ball's Bluff

Rahway River

Overlook Trail

Mines Point

Painter's Point

Beech Brook Cascades

Overlook Trail

Campbell's Pond

Lilliput Knob

Rahway Trail

WATCHUNG

Maple Falls Cascades

Pingry Trail

FIRST

Crest Trail

MOUNTAIN

Diamond Mill Pond

River Trail

Washington Rock Monument

P 9

Locust Grove Parking Area

Picnic Grove

Glen Avenue

2.0 After passing two more dams, arrive at a T intersection. Turn left (north) and cross a stone bridge onto a woods road. (**FYI:** Twenty feet to the right is the River Trail.)

2.2 Turn right (northeast) onto a trail and begin a steady climb above the Rahway River that offers a scenic view of the bottomlands.

2.8 At the trail junction turn right (east) and rock-hop across the Rahway River. On the opposite side the trail snakes its way to a bridle path. (**Option:** Continue straight [northeast] for approximately 200 yards. Turn right [east] onto the shoulder of Orange Avenue. After crossing the bridge turn right [south] onto a bridle path, traveling 200 yards to where you rejoin the Rahway Trail.)

2.9 Pass a bridle path coming in on the left (north) and continue straight (east). (**FYI:** The alternative route enters left.)

3.0 The Rahway Trail ends at the triangle, where there's a kiosk. Continue straight (southeast) onto the Lenape Trail (yellow blaze), a bridle path.

3.2 Arrive at Hemlock Falls and the turnaround spot. Via the Lenape Trail (yellow) retrace your steps (west) back to the triangle. (**Side trip:** Take the Red Dot Trail to the top of the falls for a scenic overlook of the grottos.)

3.5 At the triangle turn left (west-southwest) onto the River Trail (bridle path). (**FYI:** The route stays with the River Trail back to the Locust Grove Parking Area.)

3.6 Cross a stone bridge and continue straight, passing the Openwood Trail on your left. The path begins to ascend, arriving at a "turtleback" ledge 30 feet above the Rahway River, a good lunch spot.

3.8 Pass Ball's Bluff Trail on the left and continue straight on the path.

4.0 Pass the stone bridge and the Rahway Trail on the right and continue straight on the path. (**Reminder:** Ignore the Rahway Trail as it crosses, merges, and departs from the River Trail.)

4.7 At the triangle veer left (southeast) on the path and shortly turn right (southwest) on another path, paralleling the Rahway River. (**FYI:** The Rahway Trail [white] continues straight.)

5.8 Pass through the auto gate and arrive back at Locust Grove Parking Area.

10 State Line Lookout and the Palisades

This is a scenic out-and-back hike that runs along the top of the Palisades Cliffs above the Hudson River. There's a moderate descent and ascent on the Long Path, which uses old abandoned highways, former bridle paths, trails, and even steps to reach the State Line Boundary Monument and Station Rock. The hike provides one of the most magnificent views on the East Coast.

Distance: 1.6-mile out-and-back
Approximate hiking time: 2 hours
Difficulty/elevation gain: Easy, with only a short climb
Trail surface: Forest paths and stone steps
Best seasons: Spring through fall
Other trail users: None
Canine compatibility: Leashed dogs permitted
Permits and fees: None
Schedule: Dawn to dusk
Maps: *DeLorme New Jersey Atlas & Gazetteer*, p. 27; *USGS Yonkers, NY*, quadrangle; New York–New Jersey Trail Conference *Hudson Palisades Trails—New Jersey Section;* trail maps are also available at the park or online at www .njpalisades.org/maps.htm
Trail contacts: Palisades Interstate Park, New Jersey Section, P.O. Box 155, Alpine, NJ 07620-0155; (201) 768-1360; www .njpalisades.org
Special considerations: Inclement or icy weather cancels this hike, as many sections will be unsafe to negotiate. Think twice before bringing small children or pets on this potentially dangerous hike.

Finding the trailhead: State Line Lookout is about 1 mile south of the New York–New Jersey state line and has its own unnumbered exit from the northbound Palisades Interstate Parkway about 2 miles north of exit 2 and immediately opposite the southbound-only exit 3. From the Palisades Interstate Parkway southbound, stay in the left lane after passing exit 3. Take the U-turn (well marked). Use caution, as you will need to get into the right lane immediately to exit for State Line Lookout. The hike begins at the State Line Lookout parking area. **GPS:** N40° 59.36' / W73° 54.39'

The Hike

This walk begins at State Line Lookout, the lofty Palisades aerie that gives you a spectacular close-up of Palisades geology and great views of the ever-busy Hudson River and of Hastings-on-Hudson across the river.

If you can momentarily take your eyes off the scenery, you can ponder the political boundary that gives this spot its name. The actual state line is 0.5 mile north of here. Its long and complex history begins in 1664, when newly restored King Charles II of England gave his brother, James, duke of York, a nice present: all of New Netherland, which the English had just taken from the Dutch. The duke then gave the southerly portion of the territory (future New Jersey) to his buddies Sir George Carteret and John, Lord Berkeley. The boundary was supposed to go from 40 degrees on the Hudson River to 41 degrees 40 minutes on the Delaware River.

Problem was, the maps they had were inaccurate and unclear, and both sides tried to push the boundary as far as they could into the other guy's territory. All this made for a century of debate, controversy, confusion, political bickering, intrigue, and sometimes outright warfare. It didn't end until 1769, when the Royal Commission established the line, which was surveyed in 1774. In 1882 they re-surveyed the line, and in 1896 they figured out that both earlier surveys were wrong. Sigh.

The State Line Lookout itself reflects the handsome handiwork of two of our nation's happiest experiments in combining public relief with public works and conservation: the Civilian Conservation Corps (CCC) and the Works Progress Administration (WPA). In the 1930s the CCC employed unemployed young men in their teens and early twenties and put them to work improving America's parks and forests. The WPA generally employed adult men in larger construction projects. The roughhewn stone walls, guardrails, trails, and stone steps, as well as the rugged stone-and-timber Lookout Inn, epitomize these programs' ability to construct high-quality, long-lasting public works. They embody the richest traditions of simple, Adirondack-style park architecture. The WPA and CCC built similarly styled buildings and improvements in Palisades Interstate Park, whose traditions of rustic architecture go all the way back to the Bear Mountain Inn (built 1914).

Miles and Directions

0.0 Begin in the Lookout Inn parking lot. Head east toward Point Lookout, the Hudson River, and the retaining wall. Turn left (north) onto the Long Path (blue blaze), which is the Old 9W, an abandoned highway. The entire hike follows the Long Trail and its blue blazing.

0.2 Veer right (northeast) off the old highway and onto a woods road, following the Long Path (blue blaze).

0.6 Pass a cross-country ski trail on the left (west), a former bridle path built by the WPA in 1938.

0.7 Long Path edges a chain-link fence. Located here is the 6-foot-tall State Line Boundary Monument (built 1882),

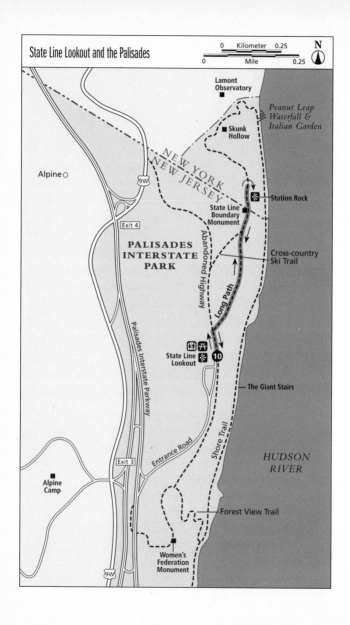

State Line Lookout and the Palisades

Kilometer
0   0.25
Mile
0   0.25

N

Lamont
Observatory

Peanut Leap
Waterfall &
Italian Garden

Skunk
Hollow

NEW YORK
NEW JERSEY

Alpine ○

9W

Station Rock

State Line
Boundary
Monument

Exit 4

PALISADES
INTERSTATE
PARK

Cross-country
Ski Trail

Abandoned Highway

Long Path

State Line
Lookout

10

The Giant Stairs

Entrance Road

Shore Trail

Exit 3

HUDSON
RIVER

Alpine
Camp

Forest View Trail

Women's
Federation
Monument

9W

Palisades Interstate Parkway

which stands 45 feet northwest down an unmarked trail. After descending stone steps, pass by open cliffs and diabase pillars.

0.8 Reach Station Rock and the turnaround point. (**FYI:** Named for the Coast and Geodetic Survey station, York. The station pin, 1 meter from the edge of the cliff, is all that remains of the bronze disk. The reference mark No.1 can be found along the trail.) Enjoy the spectacular views off the Palisades: the Hudson River, Dobbs Ferry, and the Tappan Zee Bridge.

1.6 Arrive back at the Lookout Inn parking lot. (**Option:** From the parking lot, head south on the Long Path [blue blaze] till you reach Women's Federation Monument, a castlelike structure. Here you also find "the highest cliffs . . . littered with great talus blocks" [USGS] [2.0 miles round-trip].)

11 Watchung Reservation and Blue Brook

This walk takes you on a journey through geological history, across sandstone and shale. We ramble through a deserted village and visit the Nature and Science Center, the first such exhibition in New Jersey. A special treat is passing through a grove of giant tulip trees, like New Jersey's own redwoods.

Distance: 4.7-mile loop
Approximate hiking time: 3 hours
Difficulty/elevation gain: 2 moderate climbs
Trail surface: Footpaths, woods roads, and short road walks
Best seasons: All
Other trail users: Horses on designated trails
Canine compatibility: Leashed dogs permitted
Permits and fees: None
Schedule: Dawn to dusk
Maps: *DeLorme New Jersey Atlas & Gazetteer,* p. 31; *USGS Chatham and Roselle, NJ,* quadrangles; a hiking map is also available at the reservation
Trail contacts: Union County Department of Parks and Recreation; (908) 527-4900; www .ucnj.org
Other: Paved roads that cross through the reservation are not just for park use: They are busy county roads used by commuters. Use care when crossing and keep your eyes open.

Finding the trailhead: From I-78 west, take exit 43. At the first traffic light, turn right onto McMane Avenue (CR 527). At the T intersection with Glenside Avenue, turn left. In 1.2 miles turn right onto W. R. Tracy Drive (CR 645), entering the reservation and passing multiple roads leading to picnic areas. At the traffic circle, take the first right onto Summit Lane, then turn right onto New Providence Road. The parking area is to the right, where the road makes a sharp left turn. **GPS:** N40° 40.98' / W74° 22.41'

The Hike

This hike takes us through the tranquil bottomland of the Watchungs, an oasis in an urban sea. These ridges sweep south and then west through the New Jersey Piedmont. Cradled deep within their embrace is the Great Swamp. Here the Watchungs rise like a green, rocky wave above the surrounding sea of dense urban development.

The densely forested Watchung Reservation has an aura of untouched forest that is primeval in many areas. But like most places in New Jersey, it has a long history of industrial, agricultural, and residential uses, the traces of which can be found all along our hike. It's no surprise that the first settler in this area, Peter Willcocks, dammed the Blue Brook and built a sawmill here around 1736. Felling the original forest for timber, it was soon replaced with fields, pastures, and farmsteads.

The Willcocks family also exploited another natural resource here: copper ore. The Willcocks Mine, located below the Blue Trail in Coppermine Ravine, was one of several copper mines that operated in the Watchung Mountains in the 1700s. As the original forests gave way to farmland, gristmills were added to the scene, using the waterpower of the Blue and Green Brooks to grind local grain into flour. The Willcocks family operated a gristmill on Green Brook starting around 1760.

The biggest story in the area's history came in 1844, when New York City businessman David Felt started buying up land from the Willcocks family. Felt was in the stationery business, and he soon built not just a paper mill, but also an entire community for his works nearby. The industrial village on the hillside above Blue Brook came to

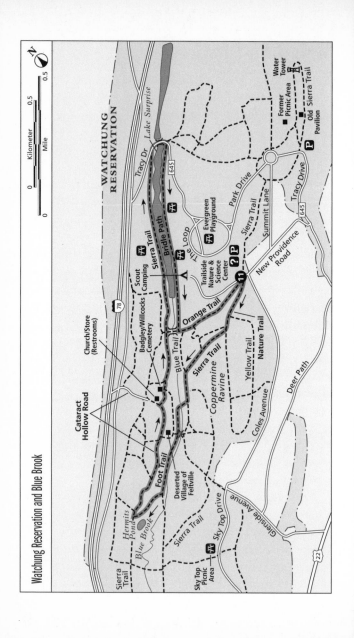

Watchung Reservation and Blue Brook

be called Feltville. The Deserted Village of Feltville, as it is now called, later became a resort community. Today it is one of the historic treasures of this part of New Jersey. Our stroll also includes traveling around Lake Surprise, surrounded in spots with tulip trees of stupendous size. It's more proof that serious wilderness exists even in the most densely populated parts of New Jersey.

Miles and Directions

0.0 From the south end of the Nature and Science Center's parking lot, locate the Sierra Trail (white blaze on an oak tree) and turn right (west) onto New Providence Road. Turn left (south) shortly onto the Nature Trail (green blaze) and proceed down the hill.

0.2 Within short order the Yellow Trail (yellow blaze) comes in from the left and becomes co-aligned with the Sierra Trail (white blaze). Turn right (north) and shortly arrive at a fork where you bear left (west) onto the Orange Trail (orange blaze), the Sierra Trail (white blaze), and the Yellow Trail. At the next fork veer left (southwest), following the Sierra Trail (white blaze) and the Yellow Trail. Finally, turn right (northwest) onto the Sierra Trail (white blaze). This maze plays out all within a very short distance!

0.6 The Blue Trail (blue blaze) enters from the right and becomes co-aligned with the Sierra Trail. (**FYI:** The Coppermine Ravine is to the left [west].)

0.7 At the bottom of the hill, the Blue Trail turns right (north). Continue straight (west) on the Sierra Trail (white blaze), crossing a streambed and shortly ascending above Blue Brook and the bottomland.

0.8 At the three-prong fork take the middle trail, leaving the Sierra Trail to bear left up the hill and the right trail to immediately drop to the bottomland. The middle trail edges the ridge above the stream before dropping down to Blue Brook.

0.9 Cross (west) Blue Brook on a rock hop and turn left (south-west) onto the trail, which meanders along the brook. (**FYI:** There is a woods road paralleling the trail on the embankment above.)

1.0 At the intersection by the bridge (left), continue straight (west) onto a bridle path, ignoring bridle paths to the left (crossing bridge) and right. (**Option:** The path to the right [northwest] leads into the Deserted Village of Feltville, entering at the 1.8-mile mark in route.)

1.3 A short distance after the path becomes mucky, turn right (northwest) and begin to ascend toward Hermit's Pond, leaving the Blue Brook bottomland. (**FYI:** Continuing straight, the bridle path becomes extremely wet, questioning whether it is a brook or a path.)

1.4 At the top of the climb, the Sierra Trail (white blaze) merges from the left (west) onto the wide path. You continue straight (east), following a wide path framed by hardwoods and spruce.

1.7 The Sierra Trail and Cataract Hollow Road (paved) become co-aligned for the next 0.3 mile, passing through the Deserted Village of Feltville.

1.8 Pass the bridle path entering on the right. (**FYI:** This is the path that connects at the 1.0-mile mark.)

1.9 Directly before the church/store (future interpretive center), turn right (northeast) onto a gravel path, following a sign leading to the historic cemetery and restrooms. A series of arrow markers lead to the cemetery.

2.0 At the T intersection turn left (northeast) and ascend the path constructed with check dams, shortly arriving at the Badgley/Willcocks family cemetery. Turn right (east) onto an earthen path, reuniting with the Sierra Trail (white blaze).

2.1 At the fork bear left (northeast), moving away from the rim of the ridge and following the Sierra Trail (white blaze). Ignore the numerous side trails.

2.3 At the T intersection the Sierra Trail turns right (east) and descends on a wide dirt road.

2.4 After a sweeping bend in the road, the Sierra Trail turns left (northeast) and *immediately* turns right (east) onto a footpath. If you miss these turns, you will come to a bridge too far.

2.6 The Sierra Trail edges Lake Surprise for less than a mile.

3.1 The Sierra Trail briefly encounters a bridle path on the left.

3.4 At CR 645 (Tracy Drive) turn right (east) onto the shoulder. Traffic is fast and furious, so care must be taken.

3.5 After crossing the auto bridge, turn right (southwest) onto the bridle path; see the signpost left of the path. The route travels the entire length of Lake Surprise, so ignore *all* paths and trails to the left (east).

4.3 At the T intersection turn left (southeast) on a "carriage road" and begin to ascend through two wooden pillars where the road and the Blue Trail are one. Avoid the section of Blue Trail leaving on the right (southwest) and continue on the "carriage road."

4.4 The "carriage road" becomes the Orange Trail. Continue straight (east), avoiding the section of the Orange Trail leaving right (southwest).

4.6 At the T intersection turn right (east) onto the shoulder of New Providence Road (closed to through traffic), ignoring all trails to the right.

4.7 Arrive back at the parking lot, which is on the left (north) side of New Providence Road.

12 The Great Swamp

Visit the former 18,000-year-old glacial Lake Passaic, now called the Great Swamp. It doesn't take long hiking this level loop to learn why it's designated a National Natural Landmark. Within the 450-acre park's natural lands, the route meanders through marshes, meadows, swamps, and woodlands, while hugging the Passaic River and series of ponds.

Distance: 2.9-mile loop
Approximate hiking time: 1.5 hours
Difficulty/elevation gain: Easy and flat
Trail surface: Paths and boardwalks
Best seasons: All
Other trail users: None
Canine compatibility: No dogs permitted
Permits and fees: None
Schedule: Dawn to dusk

Maps: *DeLorme New Jersey Atlas & Gazetteer*, p. 30–31; *USGS Bernardsville, NJ*, quadrangle; a map is also available at the park
Trail contacts: Somerset County Park Commission, 355 Milltown Rd., Bridgewater, NJ 08807; (908) 722-1200; www.somerset countyparks.org
Special considerations: Depending on the season, this serene hike could be interrupted by the mosquito.

Finding the trailhead: From I-287 in Van Dorans Mills (exit 30), turn south onto North Maple Avenue, heading toward Basking Ridge. Travel 1.7 miles to a series of traffic islands where North Maple Avenue becomes South Maple Avenue. Bear left onto South Maple Avenue (avoiding the center of the town) and travel (south) 1.0 mile. Turn left (east) onto Lord Stirling Road and go 1.5 miles. Turn left into the Environmental Education Center and the parking lot. **GPS:** N40° 41.69' / W74° 31.25'

The Hike

This hike takes us through rich bottomland meadows, once part of a glacial lake. It was prime farmland—and responsible for the park's name, indirectly. William Alexander, who lived here, was a Lord who died creating a democracy. He was born in 1725 to a wealthy family with a profitable provisioning business. He married Sarah Livingston in 1748; his brother-in-law William Livingston was a future governor. He had land interests in the East Jersey Board of Proprietors, and became one of the founders of King's College in New York, now Columbia University.

Alexander pursued a claim his family held to a lapsed Scottish earldom, which would have made him "Lord Stirling." A Scottish jury accepted the claims, but not the British House of Lords. This was still good enough for Alexander, who on his return to America in 1761 called himself "Lord Stirling." So did most everyone else, including George Washington.

With a Lord's title he decided to adopt a Lord's lifestyle. Attracted by these rich meadows here in Basking Ridge, he built a large mansion and estate, regarded at the time as one of the grandest in the colonies. At the same time, he expanded his business interests. He was heavily invested in the iron industry, and owned mines and ironworks in northern New Jersey and at Sterling Lake, New York.

All this investment lost money, and his finances grew dire. With the arrival of the Revolution, he adopted the Patriot cause, which likewise drained his finances. First a colonel in the New Jersey Militia, he later served as a general in the Continental Army; the Hessians at Trenton surrendered to him. Some regarded him as flamboyant, vain, and pompous. Others who fought alongside him called him loyal, popular with his soldiers, and brave under fire—a reliable general, if not a brilliant one.

How would this Lord fare in the new American democracy he helped create? No one knows—he died in January 1783 from chronic gout and virtually bankrupt. His property was sold to pay his debts. His grand estate fell to ruins soon after his death and was eventually forgotten.

But not forgotten forever—the site of his estate became this park, and subsequent archaeological investigations proved the grand descriptions were correct. Here you can enjoy the lovely landscape that once attracted would-be nobility.

Miles and Directions

0.0 From the northwest corner of the parking lot and the east side of the Environmental Education Center, veer right (northeast) onto the sidewalk, passing a boardwalk leaving left. Continue straight onto a gravel path leading to the trail register. Park maps are available here. Crossing the causeway, you are on the Yellow and Red Trails: Esox Pond right and Branta Pond left. (**FYI:** It's worthwhile to stop in at the interpretive center and pick up handouts and materials on flora, fauna, and history.)

0.1 Turn right (southeast) onto a grassy path. You are now solely on the Yellow Trail and will be till you reach Lenape Meadow (0.7 mile). It should also be noted that all turns will be to the right till you reach Earwig Bridge (2.0 miles). (**FYI:** Each intersection has a trail post with a map.)

0.2 At the fork (the Yellow Trail leads both ways), veer right (south) onto a grassy lane with the meadow to the right, passing a kick-out to Esox Pond.

0.3 At the fork veer right (southeast) and remain with the Yellow Trail. Ignore the lane to Lord Stirling Road and the boardwalk

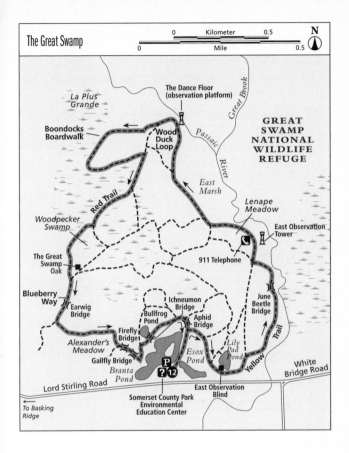

The Great Swamp

0   Kilometer   0.5

0   Mile   0.5

N

La Plus Grande

The Dance Floor (observation platform)

Great Brook

GREAT SWAMP NATIONAL WILDLIFE REFUGE

Boondocks Boardwalk

Wood Duck Loop

Passaic

Passaic River

East Marsh

Red Trail

Woodpecker Swamp

Lenape Meadow

East Observation Tower

The Great Swamp Oak

911 Telephone

Blueberry Way

Earwig Bridge

Ichneumon Bridge

Bullfrog Pond

Aphid Bridge

June Beetle Bridge

Firefly Bridge

Alexander's Meadow

Gallfly Bridge

Esox Pond

Lily Pad Pond

Yellow Trail

Branta Pond

P

? 12

White Bridge Road

Lord Stirling Road

East Observation Blind

To Basking Ridge

Somerset County Park Environmental Education Center

to Esox Pond. To your left pass the East Observation Blind and Lily Pad Pond.

0.4   At the fork veer right (east), staying with the Yellow Trail.

0.5   Pass fence and view of the Passaic River.

0.6   Cross June Beetle Bridge.

0.7   At the T intersection (Yellow Trail leads both ways), turn right (north) onto a path. Within a few hundred yards veer right (northeast) at the fork (Yellow Trail leads both ways) onto a path between the Lenape Meadow and swamp forest.

0.8 Arrive at the East Observation Tower, which overlooks the Passaic River and the Great Swamp National Wildlife Refuge. Just past this kick-out there is a 911 telephone.

0.9 At the T intersection turn right (northwest) onto a grassy lane. The route leaves the Yellow Trail and turns onto an unmarked trail, passing another unmarked trail on the left. The trail eventually becomes a boardwalk.

1.1 At the junction turn right (northeast), remaining on the boardwalk. You are hiking the Wood Duck Loop with the East Marsh on your right.

1.2 Arrive at The Dance Floor, an observation platform above the Passaic River.

1.3 Turn right (west) on a boardwalk, heading toward the Boondocks Boardwalk.

1.4 Arrive at the Boondocks Boardwalk and the La Plus Grande.

1.5 At the triangle turn right (south), remaining on a boardwalk.

1.6 Turn right (west) onto the Red Trail, remaining on a boardwalk for a short while. (**FYI:** For the remainder of the hike, the route follows the Red Trail back to the parking lot.)

1.7 Turn right (southwest) onto a path, following the Red Trail. Eventually the path becomes a boardwalk, edging Woodpecker Swamp.

1.9 Arrive at The Great Swamp Oak. At the fork veer right (southeast), staying with the Red Trail through Blueberry Way.

2.0 Cross Earwig Bridge.

2.1 Turn left (southeast) (first left turn on this hike); the trail straddles the forest and the meadow.

2.2 Ignore the Blue Trail (from Alexander's Meadow), which enters from the right, and continue straight (east), immediately crossing the Firefly Bridge. The Red Trail is co-aligned with the Blue Trail.

2.3 At the fork veer left (east), remaining on the Red Trail, and immediately cross the Gallfly Bridge. The Blue Trail departs right.

2.4 Ignore an unmarked trail (from the Hidden Marsh loop) on the left (north) and cross the Ichneumon Bridge, shortly passing Bullfrog Pond (left) and the West Observation Blind.

2.6 Ignore the unmarked trail (from the Hidden Marsh loop) on the left (north) while the trail swings east.

2.7 At the T intersection the Red Trail leads in both directions; you turn right (south) and cross the Aphid Bridge.

2.8 Ignore the Yellow Trail leaving left and continue straight on the co-aligned Red and Yellow Trails, retracing the hike from here to the parking lot.

2.9 Arrive back at the parking lot.

The Hudson River and New York Bay

In 1685 Dutch cartographer Nicolas Visscher published a map of "New Belgium," later to be called "New Netherland." It included all of present-day New York and New Jersey and prominently featured the "Groote Rivier," meaning large or great river. Also mentioned are the river's alternate names: Manhattans River, Noort (North) River, Montaigne (Mountain) River, or Mauritts River (after Prince Maurice of Nassau, Dutch royalty).

The map doesn't show the river's ultimate name, coming from an English explorer working for a Dutch trading firm. He'd first sailed up the great river seventy-five years earlier, turned around when he found it didn't go to China, and a few years later, got himself marooned way up north, never to be seen again. His name: Henry Hudson.

Hudson and his crew first explored the river in 1609, but Giovanni de Verrazano had already explored New York Bay in 1524 (and all he got was a bridge named after him). The landmarks of the lower bay were some of the first noted by European explorers. Verrazano visited Sandy Hook, as did Henry Hudson later—on maps in the 1600s they called it "Sant Punt," or Sandy Point.

New York harbor was fortified early on with lighthouses and forts, being one of the East Coast's most important ports. One of the earliest lighthouses in the nation, and the oldest still in operation, was built at Sandy Hook in 1764.

Others in the bay included the famous Little Red Light-house under the George Washington Bridge.

Though the bay was prepared for war, the greatest war-related destruction came not to any of these military fortifications, but to present-day Liberty State Park. Here, in July 1916, German saboteurs blew up the Black Tom Island munitions depot in the middle of the night. The explosion destroyed the works and spewed shrapnel for miles; many windows in lower Manhattan were blown out, and the blast woke people up in Philadelphia. As a terror attack, it was an eerie precursor to one that looms even larger at Liberty State Park: September 11, 2001, which played out in full view right across the river.

In contrast to those horrific memories, Liberty State Park is for millions of Americans the best place in the world to see the Statue of Liberty and Ellis Island, a short boat trip away. The ancestors of tens of millions of Americans passed through the Central Railroad of New Jersey Terminal here on their way from Ellis Island to their final home. This is literally America's front porch, the "Golden Door." The Hudson River and New York Bay are among the region's most scenic and historic treasures.

13 Alpine Boat Basin and the Hudson River

This spectacular out-and back hike edges the Hudson River, one of the world's major waterways. At the same time, the route travels below the massive Palisades Cliffs. A good portion of the hike traces old historic roads, while a short section runs atop a stone bulkhead (slippery when wet).

Distance: 3.4-mile lollipop
Approximate hiking time: 2.5 hours
Difficulty/elevation gain: Moderate, with gentle climbs
Trail surface: Old woods roads, trails, and rocky, uneven sea walls
Best seasons: Spring through fall
Other trail users: None
Canine compatibility: Leashed dogs permitted
Permits and fees: Yes, in season
Schedule: Dawn to dusk
Maps: New York–New Jersey Trail Conference *Hudson Palisades Map #108; USGS Yonkers, NY,* quadrangle; a map is also available from the Palisades Interstate Park Commission or online at www.njpalisades.org/maps.htm
Trail contacts: Palisades Interstate Park, New Jersey Section, P.O. Box 155, Alpine, NJ 07620-0155; (201) 768-1360; www.njpalisades.org
Special considerations: This area is likely to be quite busy on nice weekends.
Other: Keep an eye out for poison ivy, a problem here.

Finding the trailhead: From the Palisades Interstate Parkway, take exit 2 for Alpine/Closer and Route 9W South. Turn right on Alpine Approach Road and follow signs to Alpine Boat Basin. **GPS:** N40° 56.81' / W73° 55.11'

The Hike

As you travel these old roads, imagine the sites as layers of historic activities. Is your car parked where automobiles lined up to embark onto the *John Walsh* for passage to Yonkers? Or are you stepping aside for a farmer's wagon loaded with fresh vegetables, heading for the docks so his produce can be loaded onto a Hudson River sloop bound for New York City (NYC), a sloop built by shipwrights on this site? Smell the oak and cedar! Or are you catching the powerful aroma of grains being ground at the Oat Meal Mill located by the boat basin? Or do the 3,000 Sunday school children disembarking from the bunting-draped excursion barges trample you, as they scurry to be first on the merry-go-rounds? Or are you jumping from a black-powder blast from Van Sciver's quarry accompanied by the rumble of traprock being transported to the river's edge for shipment to NYC as future streets, docks, and buildings?

As you leave the river's edge on the Shore Trail, peer up at the cliffs and picture acres of forest cut for firewood, tossed from DePeyster's "pitching place." Arriving at Excelsior Flats from the Upper Trail, are you stopped by the phantom stench from the factory processing bones into fertilizer or the plant turning entrails into soap? In later years a more pleasant aroma from the Flats of grilled hotdogs and overflowing picnic baskets might greet you. If you look carefully into the undergrowth, you'll spot the ruins of the factory and remnants of the abandoned picnic area. Returning on the Shore Trail, reach Twombly's Landing where the Fresh Air Fund children (400,000 over the years) escaped the streets of NYC and arrived by steamer to enjoy Hamilton Twombly's sixty acres. His generosity did not stop there; he eventually donated this parcel to the Palisades Interstate Park, ". . . completing the task of saving the Palisades." Shortly, pass by the Excelsior Dock where the steamer *Mary Powell* let off passengers who climbed to the picnic area. River transportation was virtually the only way to Excelsior Flats. Approaching Cape Flyway (". . . a cloud-bank on the horizon, mistaken for land. . . ."), can you picture farmers' crops behind those stone terraces? In later years fishermen resided here, catching sturgeon, shad, and striped bass. Arriving back at Alpine Grove, conjure a reunion of 5,000 Grand Army of the Republic veterans and their families: Cannons roar while the band plays. After the marching and dancing, they enjoy a quiet promenade under the grove of trees, which leaves the reader to do the same.

One of the other interesting features of this walk is the Kearny House, which dates to about 1761. For generations it was called Cornwallis's Headquarters, after a nineteenth-century tradition that the famed British general had used the building when his troops disembarked and invaded New Jersey near here in November 1776. Subsequent research has cast doubts on this claim, and it's now named after James and Rachel Kearny, who lived and operated a tavern in this building here at Closter Landing in the early 1800s. Palisades Interstate Park bought the building in 1907, and in 1909 it served as the centerpiece for the opening dedication ceremonies for the new park—its birthplace! Today it interprets the history of this important riverside landing and the tavern life of the time.

A more recent architectural gem here is the Alpine Pavilion, built by the Civil Works Administration (CWA) in 1934. The CWA was a short-lived counterpart to the New Deal's Civilian Conservation Corps. This handsome

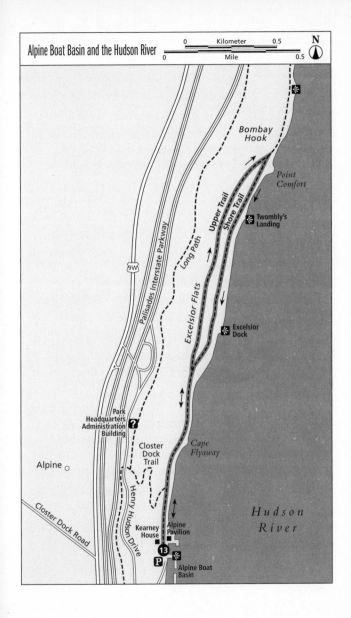

Alpine Boat Basin and the Hudson River

Kilometer 0 — 0.5
Mile 0 — 0.5

N

Bombay Hook

Point Comfort

Twombly's Landing

Upper Trail

Shore Trail

Long Path

Excelsior Flats

Excelsior Dock

9W

Palisades Interstate Parkway

Park Headquarters Administration Building

Alpine

Closter Dock Trail

Cape Flyaway

Henry Hudson Drive

Closter Dock Road

Kearney House

Alpine Pavilion

13

Alpine Boat Basin

Hudson River

stone-and-timber building reflects the classic rustic style of the era; a similar pavilion was built at the Englewood Cliffs picnic area. Enjoy it!

Miles and Directions

0.0 From the north end of the Alpine parking lot pick up the Shore Trail (white blaze), heading north on a lane. Pass a kiosk on the right and the historic Kearney House and falls on the left.

0.1 Prior to the pavilion bear left (northwest) by a blaze post and the *Old Alpine Trail* monument. Here the route begins to climb above the pavilion and the Hudson River on a semi-paved, rocky lane.

0.3 Pass the Closter Dock Trail (orange blaze) on the left (west) and continue straight on the lane.

0.6 Pass stone steps leading to Cape Flyaway and the river. Continue straight.

0.9 At the fork bear left onto the Upper Trail (no blaze), passing through the former Excelsior Flats picnic area. (**FYI:** Take note, the path bearing right, Shore Trail, is the return route.)

1.7 At the trail junctions turn right (east to south), rejoining the Shore Trail (white blaze) onto a path that has uneven rock footing and can be slippery if wet. The trail runs along the bank of the Hudson River. (**Option:** Create your own out-and-back by continuing north on the Shore Trail, which travels below the Palisade Cliffs and alongside the Hudson River.)

1.9 Pass Twombly's Landing on the left, jutting out into the river.

2.3 Reach Excelsior Dock with stone steps leading left down 30 feet to the dock. Continue south on the Shore Trail.

2.5 Pass the Upper Trail on the right and continue south on the Shore Trail, retracing the route to the Alpine parking lot.

3.4 Return to the Alpine parking lot.

14 DeKorte Park and the Meadowlands

DeKorte Park is a place of environmental renewal. This land has been diked, farmed, and lumbered; crisscrossed by turnpikes, train tracks, power lines, and pipelines. But in the last three decades, it's also become a spot dedicated to restoring native vegetation and reclaiming wildlife habitation. This extraordinary hike travels through the middle of impoundments and salt marshes along the Atlantic Flyway.

Distance: 3.7-mile loop
Approximate hiking time: 1.5 hours
Difficulty/elevation gain: Easy and flat
Trail surface: Gravel paths, floating and fixed boardwalks, and dikes
Best seasons: All, but hot in summer
Other trail users: None
Canine compatibility: Dogs not permitted
Permits and fees: None
Schedule: Mon–Fri 9 a.m.–5 p.m., Sat–Sun 10 a.m.–3 p.m.
Maps: *DeLorme New Jersey Atlas & Gazetteer,* p. 32, 78; *USGS Weehawken, NJ,* quadrangle; a map is also available at the park or online at www.meadowlands .state.nj.us/EC/come_visit/ DeKorte_Park_Map.cfm
Trail contact: Hackensack Meadowlands Environmental Center, 2 DeKorte Park Plaza, Lyndhurst, NJ 07071; (201) 460-8300; www.meadowlands .state.nj.us/ec/index.cfm

Finding the trailhead: From the New Jersey Turnpike / I-95, take exit 16W to Route 3 West. Take Route 3 West to Route 17 South (Lyndhurst exit). Follow around the ramp to the traffic light. Make a left onto Polito Avenue. Continue to the end of Polito Avenue. At the stop sign make a left onto Valley Brook Avenue. Follow this road to the end (approximately 1.5 miles). Cross the railroad tracks (keep to the left). Meadowlands Environment Center is the first building on the left after the tracks. **GPS:** N40° 47.22' / W74° 06.15'

The Hike

Most natural landscapes in New Jersey—even the wildest ones—have undergone some degree of alteration at the hand of humans. In this regard, few could hold a candle to our hike today through the Hackensack Meadowlands. This system of rivers and estuaries was once swathed in vast swamps of huge cedars, and its clear waters and wetlands were host to a wide array of wildlife.

But in the 1800s the cedar forests here fell to the ax, and the rivers were rendered salty by upstream dams, restricting freshwater flow. Original flora and fauna left the newly inhospitable environment, and new, foreign ones filled the void. The now-omnipresent phragmites reeds monopolized the wetlands. The marshlands were diked, ditched, used as trash dumps and landfills, and crisscrossed by railroads, pipelines, power lines, and highways (routes used by some of our hiking paths today). Rivers flowed not with fish, but pollution. The landscape became the evil stereotype of New Jersey: a swampy, reedy wasteland—a place to be ignored, and avoided, an abandoned, desolate, scary landscape: *Leave the gun. Take the cannoli.*

But with the growth of the environmental movement in the 1960s, the Meadowlands were recognized not as worthless, but as a natural environment that was once magnificent and that could be again. It was also recognized as an important wildlife habitat: Some 265 bird species make their home in the park. Dozens others migrate through here, making it a major stop on the Atlantic Flyway. Some past damage can never be repaired, but after decades of concerted efforts, the Hackensack Meadowlands are now rebounding in a big way.

With land acquisition and restoration, the Meadowlands are poised to become one of the great wild urban greenways of the world—a green oasis in the shadow of the Manhattan skyline. Enjoy this walk through marshlands and reed-forests; at times, only the glimpse of the top of a skyscraper will tell you that you're practically next to Manhattan.

Miles and Directions

0.0 From the southwest end of the parking lot, locate the entrance to the Meadowlands Environmental Center.

0.3 The Kingsland Overlook Trail ends at the entrance road. Cross (southeast) it and proceed onto a brick walkway, which leads to the Marsh Discovery trailhead. Take the Marsh Discovery Trail into Kingsland Tidal Impoundment via a floating boardwalk.

0.8 At the T intersection turn right (northwest) onto the Transco Trail (yellow blaze). (**Side trip:** Turn left [southeast] onto the Transco Trail for an out-and-back.)

1.2 The Transco Trail intersects the Shorewalk (right) and the path leading (left) to Lyndhurst Nature Reserve. Continue straight (northwest).

1.8 The Transco Trail swings left (west) before the road and through a sitting area. At the junction the Transco Trail terminates. Turn left (south) onto Saw Mill Creek Trail (blue blaze), passing through an elaborate wrought iron gate.

2.2 As the trail moves through a gate, pass the Saw Mill Creek Trail Extension to your left and continue straight. (**FYI:** The hike will return via the extension, so make a mental note of the spot.)

2.8 Cross over a bridge and arrive at a chain link fence, your

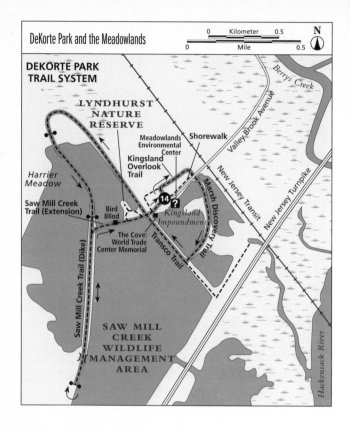

turnaround point. Retrace the hike back to the Saw Mill
Creek Trail Extension, before the gate.

3.3 Turn right (east) onto the Saw Mill Creek Trail Extension
(blue blaze).

3.4 Proceed through a bird blind and arrive at the Lyndhurst
Nature Reserve. (**Side trip:** The two paths on the left create
a loop into the reserve.)

3.5 The Saw Mill Creek Trail Extension terminates at the intersection with the Transco Trail and Shorewalk. Continue straight

onto the Shorewalk, which is a stroll along the sidewalk, passing an impressive World Trade Center Memorial, a sculpture silhouette of the Manhattan skyline, and Meadow Commission courtyard.

3.7 Arrive back at the Meadowlands Environmental Center's entrance and the parking lot.

15 Liberty State Park and New York Bay

On this walk the skyline isn't broken by towering oaks, sycamore, or white pines, but by Lady Liberty, Columbus Monument, the Liberation Monument, and Manhattan skyscrapers. The route takes advantage of walkways, the nature path, the Interpretive Center, the Central Railroad of New Jersey Terminal, and especially the Liberty Walk. All these border salt marshes, coves, ponds, the Hudson River, and the Morris Canal Big Basin. It's all bustling with bicycles, yachts, tugs, helicopters, and multinational sightseers.

Distance: 5.1-mile loop
Approximate hiking time: 3 hours
Difficulty/elevation gain: Easy and flat
Trail surface: Walkways, paths, and sidewalks
Best seasons: All
Other trail users: Bicyclists
Canine compatibility: Leashed dogs permitted
Permits and fees: None
Schedule: Dawn to dusk

Maps: *DeLorme New Jersey Atlas & Gazetteer,* p. 33, 81; *USGS Jersey City, NJ,* quadrangle; a map is also available at the park or online at www.getnj.com/lsp/lspmaps.shtml
Trail contacts: Liberty State Park, Morris Pesin Dr., Jersey City, NJ 07305; (201) 915-3440; www.state.nj.us/dep/parksandforests/parks/liberty.html

Finding the trailhead: From the juncture of I-95 and I-78 in Newark, travel east on I-78 (also called New Jersey Turnpike Extension), crossing the Newark Bay Bridge. Take exit 14B (Jersey City/Liberty State Park). From the tollbooth bear left and then turn left onto Bay View Avenue, all the while following Liberty State Park signs. Travel 0.2 mile till you come to a rotary. Take the first exit from the circle onto Morris Pesin Drive, taking it 0.7 mile through the entrance to the park and following it to the third and final parking lot on your right (just past Freedom Way on the left). The park office, restrooms, and concession are at the southeast end of the parking lot. **GPS:** N40° 41.70' / W74° 03.54'

The Hike

This hike takes us past the historic Morris Canal Basin, the world's best view of Manhattan, a spectacular historic train shed and railroad terminal, views of Ellis Island and the Statue of Liberty, and the site of an infamous island munitions depot. The famous Morris Canal connected with the bay in the canal basin on the north side of the park here. Later, the Central Railroad of New Jersey (CRRNJ) built a rail terminal and depot. By the Civil War it was a hub of industry and transportation.

Nearby stands the Statue of Liberty on Liberty Island (formerly Bedloe's Island). First proposed in 1871, the statue, a gift from France to the United States, rapidly became one of the great American icons. More activity came to the area in 1892, when immigration processing was transferred from Manhattan to a new immigration facility on nearby Ellis Island. From the time it opened in 1892 until it closed in 1954, some seventeen million immigrants entered the United States via Ellis Island. The present landmark immigration building was built in 1900, replacing an earlier building.

Black Tom Island, originally linked to the mainland by a causeway here, was used to store munitions being shipped to Europe, where World War I was raging. By July 1916 it is estimated some two million pounds of explosives were cached on the island. This was a tempting target for Ger-

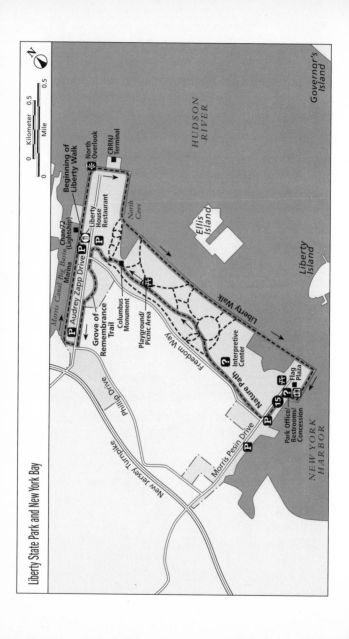

Liberty State Park and New York Bay

N

0   0.5   Kilometer
0   0.5   Mile

Morris Canal Big Basin, Chan//72
Marina
Beginning of Liberty Walk
North Overlook
CRRNJ Terminal
Liberty House Restaurant
North Cove
Audrey Zapp Drive
Grove of Remembrance Trail
Columbus Monument
Playground/Picnic Area
Freedom Way
Nature Path
Interpretive Center
Philip Drive
Morris Pesin Drive
New Jersey Turnpike
Park Office/Restrooms/Concession
Flag Plaza
Liberty Walk
HUDSON RIVER
Governor's Island
Ellis Island
Liberty Island
NEW YORK HARBOR

15

man saboteurs. In the early hours of July 30, 1916, the island went *kaboom*—to put it mildly. The explosion registered something like 5.5 on the Richter scale and caused over $20 million in damage in the greater Jersey City/Manhattan area. The area between Black Tom Island and the rail terminal to the north was ultimately filled in; former Black Tom Island is now the area at the end of Morris Pesin Drive.

Tragically, it wasn't the last time foreign terrorists brought destruction and mayhem to this area: The World Trade Center was scarcely a mile across the Hudson.

The shadows of past tragedy can't dampen the generally ebullient atmosphere at Liberty State Park, however. It's often a busy and bustling park, the crowds a reminder of the days when the tired, the poor, the huddled masses yearning to breathe free passed through here. As brand-new Americans they got the world's best welcome by the lady in the harbor, her torch held high as a beacon, guiding them to a better life.

Miles and Directions

0.0 Begin the hike by walking to the north end of the parking lot and proceed out the entrance. Cross (northeast) Morris Pesin Drive and onto the paved walkway paralleling Freedom Way, a road that borders the undeveloped section of the park.

0.2 Turn right (southeast) onto the brick Nature Path.

0.3 Arrive at the Interpretive Center. Turn left (northwest) and within 40 feet turn right (northeast) before Freedom Way and onto the paved walkway.

0.4 After passing a gravel road on the right (not shown on the park map), turn right (east) onto a paved walkway where you begin to have a spectacular wide-open view of Ellis Island, the Statue of Liberty, and the Big Apple.

0.5 Ascend (east) up a grade to a brick-laid patio. Proceed directly across the circle to a T intersection; turn left (northeast) onto a paved walkway. General directions: Proceed straight (northeast) up the middle of the park on the paved path, ignoring the numerous intersections, which lead to either Freedom Way (left) or Liberty Walk (right).

0.7 Pass through a circular garden and continue straight (northeast) on the walkway.

1.0 Pass through a picnic area with restrooms, drinking water, telephones, and playground. Continue straight (north) on the walkway.

1.1 Pass Columbus Monument. (**Side trip:** Turn right [southeast] to explore the monument and the North Cove.)

1.2 Just before Freedom Way at the T intersection, turn right (northeast) onto a walkway. (**FYI:** You are now passing the former sheds of the Central Railroad of New Jersey [CRRNJ].)

1.3 Just before Audrey Zapp Drive (cobblestone), turn left (west) crossing Freedom Way and onto a walkway paralleling Audrey Zapp Drive. Immediately turn left (south) into the east entrance to the Millennium Park/Grove of Remembrance loop and work your way west toward Phillip Drive.

1.8 Arrive at Phillip Drive where the Grove of Remembrance Trail ends. Turn right and cross (north) Audrey Zapp Drive through a lot and down a culvert to the Liberty Landing Marina walkway. Turn right (east) onto the path, putting the Morris Canal Big Basin on your left.

2.7 Pass *Chan/72*, a lightship, on your left, and the Liberty House, a restaurant, on your right. The Liberty Walk path, which runs along the bulkhead, also begins here.

2.8 Pass the North Overlook and the Liberty Walk turns right (south), placing the Hudson River to your left (east).

2.9 Pass the CRRNJ Terminal and continue south. (**Side trip:**

Free. Explore the interior of the terminal [an industrial cathedral] and visit the small museum. Restrooms are also available.) (**FYI:** You can access ferry service to the Statue of Liberty and Ellis Island from this spot for a fee and a security check.)

3.0 Turn right (northwest) and continue to edge the Hudson River.

3.1 Climb the stairs where the Liberty Walk veers left (west) onto a causeway between the Hudson River and the North Cove. General directions: Head southwest on Liberty Way (bulk-head), ignoring the numerous paths coming in on the right.

4.8 Arrive at the end of Liberty Way. Turn right (northwest) onto a walkway, which continues to run along the edge of the bulkhead.

4.9 Pass Liberation Monument on the right. Shortly pass the Flag Plaza on the right.

5.0 Turn right (northeast) on the walkway, bordering the water and the picnic area. (**FYI:** This is the area of the Black Tom disaster.)

5.1 Arrive back at the park office, restrooms, concession stand, and the parking lot.

16 The Delaware and Raritan Canal– Millstone Valley

This loop is a good level hike for a spring warm-up or a Sunday afternoon stroll. While sauntering under a canopy of trees, enjoy the rushing river on one side and the placid canal on the other. The hike affords numerous interpretive kiosks and side trips to the historical sites. Easy to add more miles!

Distance: 3.8-mile loop
Approximate hiking time: 2 hours
Difficulty/elevation gain: Easy and flat
Trail surface: Towpath and railroad bed
Best seasons: All
Other trail users: Multiuse trail
Canine compatibility: Leashed dogs permitted
Permits and fees: None
Schedule: Dawn to dusk
Maps: *DeLorme New Jersey Atlas & Gazetteer* p. 42; *USGS Hightstown* and *Monmouth Junction, NJ,* quadrangles. Maps and charts are also available at the park and online at www.dandr canal.com/maps.html.
Trail contacts: D & R Canal State Park, 625 Canal Road, Somerset 08873; (732) 873-3050; www.state.nj.us/dep/ parksandforests/parks/drcanal .html. Delaware and Raritan Canal Commission, P.O. Box 539, Highway 29, Prallsville Mills, Stockton 08559; (609) 397-2000; www.dandrcanal .com/index.html
Special considerations: Lots of poison ivy here. Beware.

Finding the trailhead: From the intersection of US 206 and NJ 27 in Princeton, travel 3.1 miles north on NJ 27, where you will cross a bridge over the Millstone River. Turn right into the Delaware and Raritan Canal State Park parking lot (just before a bridge over the canal). GPS: N40° 22.45' / W74° 37.14'

The Hike

This hike begins at the Crossroads of New Jersey. During the Late Woodland Period, the Lenape's Assunpink Trail took advantage of the Millstone Valley floodplain running between the Delaware and Raritan Rivers. In the mid-1600s the Dutch used it to travel between New Amsterdam and the Dutch settlements along the Delaware Bay. Later, the Old Dutch Trail became the British Kings Highway, connecting New York City with Philadelphia. In 1913 the Kings Highway was designated as the Lincoln Highway, patching together other roads to create the first transcontinental route, thus promoting the use of the automobile. The Lincoln Highway passed through twelve states from New York City to San Francisco.

Opened in 1834, the Delaware and Raritan Canal (DRC) is a 75-foot-wide (top) / 60-foot-wide (bottom) by 8-foot-deep water route that uses fourteen locks to create a 36-mile shortcut between the Delaware and Raritan Rivers. It connected Philadelphia with New York City and the Pennsylvania anthracite-coal fields with Hudson Valley. The canal operations lasted nearly a hundred years, with barges pulled by mules and eventually steam tugs. The DRC's golden years straddled the 1860s to the 1870s, carrying more tonnage in a single year (1871) than the celebrated Erie Canal. Currently, the canal acts as a water supply for Central Jersey.

Your hike takes the towpath from Kingston to Rocky Hill. Crossing the bridge over the canal, your return route uses the other industrial road: the Rocky Hill Railroad, a branch of the Camden and Amboy Railroad (the first chartered railroad in the United States). The spur, along with the canal, carried decorative tile, shrubs and nursery plants, and traprock throughout the country. Nevertheless, the rail met its demise in the early 1970s.

Today, your hike is officially on the National Recreation Trail as well as the East Coast Greenway, a crossroads of not only those who recreate but also the linear corridor for the migrations of plants and animals.

Miles and Directions

0.0 From the southwest end of the parking lot, pick up the macadam path and pass (north) through the tunnel under NJ 27, ascending onto the towpath. The Millstone River is on the left and the Delaware & Raritan Canal on the right.

0.3 Pass concrete milemarker. (**FYI:** The number 24 is the canal miles to New Brunswick, and the number 20 is the canal miles to Bordentown, for a grand total of 44 miles on the main canal.)

0.6 Pass along the spillway of the canal with a series of canal relative interpretive kiosks. (**FYI:** The spillway acted as flood prevention for the canal, sending the excess water into the Millstone River.)

1.9 At the junction with Georgetown-Franklin Turnpike (CR 518), turn right (east) and cross the bridge over the canal; turn right again onto the rail bed of the Camden & Amboy Railroad, passing through a historical site. Just beyond it is a parking lot with restrooms. The infamous trap quarry can be seen and heard east of the rail grade. Plan on spending a little time among the "ruins" and reading the interpretive kiosks.

2.4 Pass a bench and a trail (blue blazes) on the left and continue straight on the rail bed. (**Side trip:** Take the blue-blazed trail left and ascend the ridge for 0.125 mile to historic Rockingham, the mansion where George Washington spent three months waiting for the Treaty of Paris to

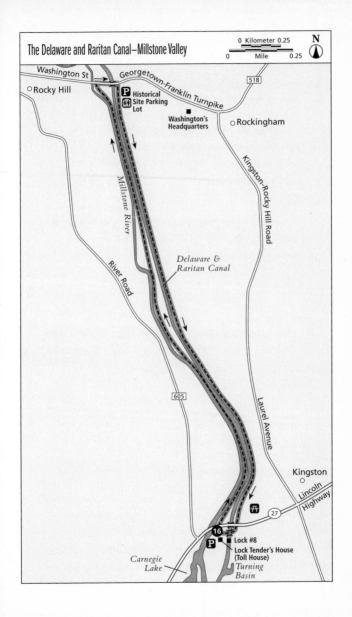

The Delaware and Raritan Canal–Millstone Valley

N

0 Kilometer 0.25
0 Mile 0.25

Washington St
Georgetown-Franklin Turnpike
518

Rocky Hill

P Historical
Site Parking
Lot

Washington's
Headquarters

Rockingham

Kingston-Rocky Hill Road

Millstone River

Delaware &
Raritan Canal

River Road

605

Laurel Avenue

Kingston

Lincoln
Highway
27

16
P Lock #8
Lock Tender's House
(Toll House)

Carnegie
Lake

Turning
Basin

be signed, ending the American Revolution. Local lore says Washington gave his farewell address to his troops from the balcony of Rockingham.)

3.7 The trail swings away from the canal and into a picnic area. Pass through the parking lot till you arrive at NJ 27. Cross it and turn right (west) into the park entrance and immediately cross the canal, arriving back into the parking lot. (**Side trip:** Continue south on the towpath, passing Lock #8, and arrive at Millstone Aqueduct, footbridge, and Carnegie Lake. Round-trip adds about 0.6 mile. This was the halfway point on the canal, and it became a layover spot for canal traffic. This was also a busy place for the canal tender; he had to open and shut the locks, swing open or close the bridge, and collect the toll!)

3.8 Arrive back at parking lot.

17 Cheesequake State Park

Though close to the Garden State Parkway and the metropolis, the terrain here in Cheesequake State Park is pleasantly diverse and rather remote. Journey past historic clay pits along with an array of ecosystems: saltwater marshes, freshwater swamps, white cedar swamps, hardwood forests, and pine barrens. A bit hilly, the loop hike is made up of trails, stairs, boardwalks, and park roads. Be aware that the park has a limited capacity and closes when full.

Distance: 4.5-mile loop

Approximate hiking time: 2.5 hours

Difficulty/elevation gain: Moderately easy

Trail surface: Trails, stairs, boardwalks, and roads

Best seasons: All

Other trail users: Multiuse

Canine compatibility: Leashed dogs permitted

Permits and fees: Yes, in season

Schedule: Dawn to dusk

Maps: *DeLorme New Jersey Atlas & Gazetteer*, p. 38; *USGS South Amboy, NJ*, quadrangle; a map is also available at the park

Trail contacts: Cheesequake State Park, 300 Gordon Rd., Matawan, NJ 07747; (702) 566-2161; www.state.nj.us/dep/parksandforests/parks/cheesequake.html

Finding the trailhead: From Garden State Parkway southbound, take exit 120 to Laurence Harbor/Matawan, Cheesequake State Park. In 0.3 mile keep bearing right (south) onto Matawan Road/Laurence Harbor Parkway (Middlesex County Road 626). In 0.2 mile turn right (west) onto Morristown Road (Middlesex County Road 689). In 0.3 mile turn right (north) onto Gordon Road and drive 0.6 mile to the Cheesequake State Park Contact Station. Passing the park office on the right, travel 0.1 mile on the park road to the trailhead parking lot on the left. **GPS:** N40° 26.16' / W74° 15.95'

The Hike

This hike through Cheesequake State Park highlights how different centuries see value in different things. For us, the area is a beautiful, amazing transition zone: from the hilly, forested Piedmont to the sandy pine barrens of the Coastal Plain—also from the saltwater bay and marshes to the freshwater swamps and creeks. But Colonial craftsmen saw something else—rich yellow clay in the riverbanks that's abundant and superior for stoneware pottery. Central New Jersey played an important role in Colonial American pottery manufacture. It had good transportation, skilled labor, and an entrepreneurial climate. These wouldn't have meant much without this band of clay deposits running from Perth Amboy to Trenton. With this geological leg up, potteries sprang up throughout the region.

An important pottery was here in the Cheesequake area (then South Amboy) established by Captain James Morgan ca. 1770. The Morgan Pottery produced a variety of handsome and decorative kiln-fired household stoneware, including bowls, jugs, crocks, jars, beer mugs, plates, colanders, and other goods. Morgan died ca. 1784, and the pottery works were taken over by his son-in-law Thomas Warne, who later joined with *his* son-in-law Joshua Letts. The Warne & Letts Pottery became even better known than Morgan's. Warne & Letts ceased production about 1827. Gone, but hardly forgotten today: Cheesequake-area stoneware produced by Morgan and Warne & Letts is now highly collectible. Indeed, most surviving Morgan pieces are in museums, and the rare ones that come up for sale fetch four and five figures. Could the farm wives of long ago have dreamt that the cider jug in their hands, bought for a dollar, would someday be worth $15,000? Probably not, or they wouldn't have dropped so many . . .

Cheesequake's clay industry didn't end there—Harry C. Perrine & Sons Co. of South Amboy continued to mine clay in the twentieth century, from about 1900 to 1918, and again in the 1940s and 1950s. This legacy is reflected in place names along our hike—Perrine's Road and Perrine Pond, a former clay-mining pit now filled with water. Cheesequake State Park opened in 1940.

Miles and Directions

0.0 Locate the trailhead kiosk at the southwest corner of the parking lot. Head west onto the Yellow, Green, Red, Blue, and White Trails. Shortly, before a set of stairs, veer right onto the Yellow Trail (loop, yellow blaze), which runs the crest of the knoll.

0.3 The trail descends. Before reaching the bottom of the stairs, turn left (south) onto a trail (yellow blaze) with the salt marsh on the right, leading away from the beach.

0.7 Turn right (south) onto the Red Trail, which is now co-aligned with the Blue and Green Trails. Immediately cross a wooden bridge and ascend a steep grade, heading toward the Interpretive Center.

0.8 Arrive at the Interpretive Center. Pick up the Blue Trail to the right (west) of the front of the building and head southwest. (The Blue Trail is co-aligned with the Red and Green Trails.) (**Side trip:** Explore the local displays in the center.)

0.9 At the T intersection at the top of the stairs, turn right (north) onto the Blue Trail, leaving the Red and Green Trails. Run the ridge before dropping down into the salt marsh.

1.1 Cross a 325-foot boardwalk above the salt marsh.

1.2 Pass a clay pit on the left.

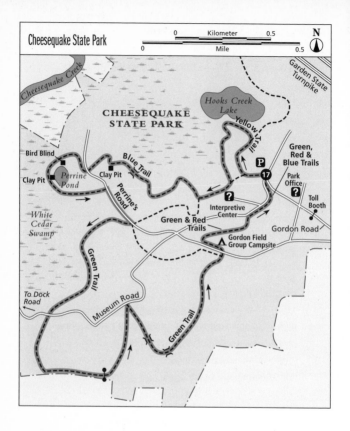

Cheesequake State Park

1.3 At the T intersection turn right (north) onto Perrine's Road. Shortly you encounter a fork in the road; veer left (west) onto a sandy road, continuing on the Blue Trail.

1.5 Arrive at Perrine Pond and a bird blind. (**FYI:** The pond was formally a clay pit.)

1.8 At the T intersection turn right (southeast) onto Perrine's Road and into some shade.

2.0 At the trail junction make a sharp right turn (west) onto the Green Trail (green blaze). (**Bailout:** Continue straight on Perrine's Road. Turn left (east) onto Museum Road and back to the parking lot (0.8 mile).

2.3 Arrive at a freshwater swamp. Continue along the boardwalk (slippery when wet!).

2.5 Arrive at an imposing American white cedar swamp.

2.7 Cross (south) Museum Road and move under some impressive white pines. (**Side trip:** Turning right onto Museum Road and right on Dock Road brings you to the former steamboat landing and views of Cheesequake Creek [Round-trip: 1.4 miles].) (**Bailout:** Turn left onto Museum Road and back to the parking lot [1.1 miles].)

2.8 The Green Trail bears left (southeast) and begins climbing through pines and hardwoods, crossing a series of bridges.

3.0 Before a gate, the trail swings left (northeast) and passes a vernal swamp on the right before descending through a trench.

3.3 The Green Trail swings right (east), descending, skirting a floodplain, and avoiding the sandy road.

4.0 At the T intersection turn left (north) onto Perrine's Road, passing Gordon Field Group Campsite. Just beyond the "Comfort Station" (seasonal), turn right (northeast) onto the Green Trail and the Red Trail, skirting the campground.

4.3 At the T intersection turn right (east) onto Museum Road (the Blue, Red, and Green Trails) and follow it to the parking lot. (On the way, you pass the entrance to the Interpretive Center.)

4.5 Arrive back at the parking lot.

18 Sandy Hook

Starting at a historic Life–Saving Station, now a museum, we explore the thickets, the dunes, and the shore of the Sandy Hook section of Gateway National Recreation Area. Stroll along the Atlantic Ocean and pass a freshwater pond (great for birding) and an old Nike missile base. A little bit of everything!

Distance: 3.8-mile figure 8
Approximate hiking time: 2 hours
Difficulty/elevation gain: Easy
Trail surface: Pathways, sandy trails, sidewalks, and beach
Best seasons: All
Other trail users: Multiuse
Canine compatibility: No dogs on the beach; otherwise leashed dogs permitted
Permits and fees: Yes
Schedule: Dawn to dusk
Maps: *DeLorme New Jersey Atlas & Gazetteer*, p. 39; *USGS Sandy Hook, NJ*, quadrangle; maps are also available at the recreation area or online at www.nps.gov/gate/shu/shu_maps_directions.htm
Trail contacts: Sandy Hook Visitor's Center, Gateway National Recreation Area, P.O. Box 530, Fort Hancock, NJ 07732; (732) 872-5970; www.nps.gov/gate/shu/shu_home.htm
Special considerations: Be forewarned: Crowds, mosquitoes, ticks, and poison ivy are part of the summertime fun; you might want to consider the off-season. If the park would knock back the poison ivy, this would be one of New Jersey's most exciting hikes.
Other: It's easy to add miles to this hike for a longer stroll.

Finding the trailhead: From NJ 36 in Highlands, get on Ocean Avenue. Take Ocean Avenue for 0.3 mile to the Entrance Plaza; it becomes Hartshorne Drive. From the toll plaza travel 2 miles on Harthshorne Drive to the Sandy Hook Visitor Center where the hike begins. **GPS:** N40° 25.61' / W73° 59.09'

The Hike

Some of our parks and historic sites are "accidental" ones—for most of their existence they weren't valued for culture or recreation, but for practical reasons. A perfect example is Sandy Hook, the location of this hike. European sailors first entered New York harbor some five centuries ago. The great sandy point that extends north from the mainland across the harbor entrance—Sandy Hook—has always been a barrier. The bay is wide here, but the historic shipping channel required a treacherously close squeeze against Sandy Hook—you could toss a biscuit from a ship and hit it, so it was said.

The dangers of this harbor entrance led Colonial New York shipping and mercantile interests to lobby for the erection of a lighthouse here. Sandy Hook lighthouse was built and first lit in 1764. The unique flat-sided structure is now the oldest lighthouse in America, and still in use. In the 1840s another effort to safeguard shipping was made with the creation of a U.S. Life-Saving Station here. These stations were charged with rescuing passengers from foundering ships off the coast. One of these Life-Saving Stations is now the park's visitor center.

These efforts made the harbor entrance safer for ships, but not *all* ships are friendly. Sandy Hook also had military importance. Both British and American troops were, at different times, stationed around the lighthouse during the Revolutionary War, but it wasn't until the War of 1812 that this strategic point saw construction of a military installation. Fort Gates, a temporary fortification, was built to guard New York against the British Navy. In 1817 the federal government bought Sandy Hook peninsula in its entirety, and in 1859 started construction of a permanent fort made of granite. But the development of the rifled-bore cannon, which could punch through the thickest masonry, made such forts obsolete, and it was never finished.

By the early 1950s, the notion of defending harbors with artillery was obsolete, and antiaircraft guns were replaced with Nike Air Defense Missiles. These were designed to intercept and destroy enemy warplanes before they reached New York City. There were two types: the Nike Ajax, used in the 1950s, which had a range of 30 miles, and the Nike Hercules, used from the late 1950s until 1974, which had a nuclear warhead and a range of over 100 miles. You'll get to see a (disarmed!) Nike missile on our hike.

In the 1960s and 1970s the focus of defense shifted yet again from jet aircraft to nuclear missiles, and Fort Hancock once again found itself outmoded. In 1974 the Army deactivated Fort Hancock. Happily, the property was transferred to the National Park Service to become part of the new Gateway National Recreation Area. The entire peninsula was designated a National Historic Landmark in 1982. As a historic site, it reflects an array of military technology from the 1850s through the 1950s, and is rich in architectural treasures.

Miles and Directions

0.0 From the Sandy Hook Visitor Center locate the OLD DUNE TRAIL sign on the north end of the parking lot and turn onto the trail. (**FYI:** The center, once a Duluth-style Life-Saving Station [1894], is a National Historical Landmark. It is also a museum with restrooms, open daily 10 a.m.–5 p.m.)

0.2 Cross (north) the entrance road to South Beach Area E and venture through a thicket before crossing (east) the Multi-Use Pathway and onto a sandy trail.

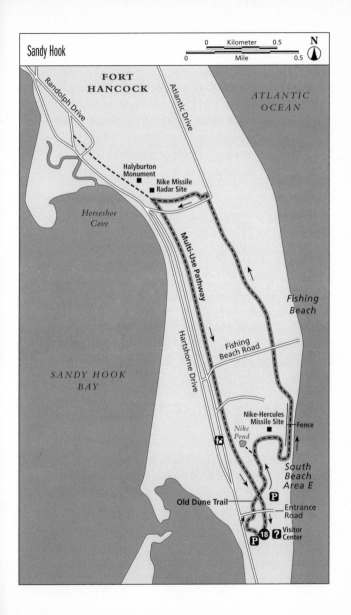

Sandy Hook

FORT HANCOCK

ATLANTIC OCEAN

Randolph Drive

Atlantic Drive

Halyburton Monument

Nike Missile Radar Site

Horseshoe Cove

Multi-Use Pathway

Fishing Beach

Hartshorne Drive

Fishing Beach Road

SANDY HOOK BAY

Nike-Hercules Missile Site

Fence

Nike Pond

South Beach Area E

Old Dune Trail

P

Entrance Road

P 18

Visitor Center

0.3 Arrive at the interpretive kiosk, Old Salty Survivors, and continue straight (north).

0.4 Arrive at the observation platform. (**Side trip:** Left of the platform, take a short journey via the path and boardwalk to a blind overlooking Nike Pond, a freshwater pond.)

0.5 Arrive at the Nike Missile Site kiosk and turn right (south) onto a sandy path.

0.6 The trail swings east, crossing the primary dunes.

0.7 Arrive at the Atlantic Ocean; turn left (north) and head up the beach.

1.0 Keep your eyes on the missile-site fence to the west. One hundred yards beyond the last fence pole and by a nondescript trail post, turn left (west) back through the primary dunes and into the secondary dunes. There will be a series of trail posts, but even so, it is a bit of a maze through the dunes and thickets. (**FYI:** This left turn is before Fishing Beach, dotted with fishermen.)

1.3 Arrive at Fishing Beach Road. Cross (north) the pavement, picking up the trail by the SOUTH BEACH DUNE TRAIL sign. Continue to follow trail posts with arrows through the maze of trails.

2.0 Pass around a cabled gate and arrive at Atlantic Drive. Cross by zigzagging west then north, picking up the trail by the SPEED LIMIT 35 sign. (**Option:** If the trail becomes poison ivy choked, you may opt to take the shoulder of Atlantic Drive west to the Multi-Use Pathway.)

2.2 At the T intersection turn left (south) onto the Multi-Use Pathway, a paved lane. Shortly cross Atlantic Drive. (**Option:** If the black pavement is too hot, turn around and retrace route.) (**FYI:** The multiuse pathway is the return route.)

2.9 Cross Fishing Beach Road.

3.0 Cross the road leading to South Maintenance (former Nike base). To the right and across Hartshorne Drive is a historic Nike Ajax missile.

3.2 Pass the ranger station.

3.5 Cross the Old Dune Trail, with South Beach Area E on the left. Cross the entrance road to the parking lot.

3.8 Arrive at the Sandy Hook Visitor Center parking lot.

Hike Alternatives

Here are a few suggestions for other good, relatively easy hike possibilities. Consult maps and park agencies for details.

1   Jockey Hollow and Morristown National Historical Park
2   Bearfort Ridge, Wawayanda State Park
3   Skylands Botanical Gardens
4   Ramapo Mountain State Forest—Millstone Hill
5   Garrett Mountain Reservation
6   Eagle Rock Reservation
7   Apshawa Preserve
8   Branch Brook Park
9   Ramapo Mountain Reservation—Havermeyer Hollow and Green Mountain Valley
10   Terrace Pond
11   Great Swamp National Wildlife Refuge

Clubs and Trail Groups

New York-New Jersey Trail Conference
156 Ramapo Valley Rd. (Route 202)
Mahwah, NJ 07430
(201) 512-9348
www.nynjtc.org/contact.html

Adirondack Mountain Club
814 Goggins Rd.
Lake George, NY 12845
(518) 668-4447
www.adk.org

The Appalachian Mountain Club
5 Joy St.
Boston, MA 02108
(617) 523-0655
www.outdoors.org

Appalachian Trail Conservancy
799 Washington St.
P.O. Box 807
Harpers Ferry, WV 25425-0807
(304) 535-6331
www.appalachiantrail.org

Green Mountain Club
4711 Waterbury-Stowe Rd.
Waterbury Center, VT 05677
(802) 244-7037
www.greenmountainclub.org

New Jersey Audubon Society
9 Hardscrabble Rd.
Bernardsville, NJ 07924
(908) 204-8998
www.njaudubon.org

About the Authors

Paul E. DeCoste is a native of New Jersey, brought up in a hiking family. As a nipper, he explored Mount Tammany, traversed the ice-covered Great Swamp, vacationed on Cape May Point, and tramped about Jockey Hollow on Sunday afternoons. As a member of the New York–New Jersey Trail Conference, he became part of the New Jersey volunteer management team for the Appalachian Trail, relocating it through the Great Valley and up the Wawayanda Mountain. He created and taught "Take a Hike" and "Appalachian Trail as an Educational Resource," encouraging folks to utilize the New Jersey park systems. A graduate of East Stroudsburg and Drew Universities, he taught for thirty years within the Garden State. Married with two children, he resides in Sussex County.

Ronald J. Dupont Jr. is a lifelong resident of northwestern New Jersey and a 1985 graduate of Columbia College, Columbia University. Over the last two decades, he has written three books and numerous articles on history in Sussex County and northern New Jersey. A Life Member of the New York–New Jersey Trail Conference, he is a longtime trail maintainer in High Point State Park. Among other trail-related activities, he prepared a historical and archaeological survey of the Appalachian Trail in New Jersey for the New Jersey Management Committee of the Appalachian Trail Conference. Married with two children, he lives in Highland Lakes, New Jersey.